60p

MICHAEL BARRATT'S
down-to-earth
gardening
book

MICHAEL BARRATT'S
down-to-earth gardening book

Patrick Stephens, Cambridge,
in association with Garden News Limited

First edition October 1974

ISBN 0 85059 198 8

Typeset in Helvetica by Blackfriars Press Ltd,
Leicester.
Printed on 115 gsm Nimrod Cartridge by
Jayprint Ltd, Thurmaston, Leicester.
Bound by Hunter & Foulis Ltd, Edinburgh,
Scotland.
Published by Patrick Stephens Limited, Bar
Hill, Cambridge, CB3 8EL, in association with
Garden News Limited, 117 Park Road,
Peterborough, PE1 2TS.

Contents

Introduction

Why will no one believe me?

Ever since I took over as question master of BBC radio's *Gardeners' Question Time,* and subsequently started a weekly column in *Garden News,* I've been trying to convince the dual audience that I'm Britain's most ignorant gardening expert. But people just smile indulgently and think I'm joking.

I'm not, I'm really not!

Perhaps the following pages will convince you of how little I know about horticultural matters. At the same time, I hope that we'll both be a great deal more knowledgeable by the time we come to the last page.

We've tried to get back to basics, so the advice from my specialist friends covers fundamentals like how fertilisers and composts work, how to propagate plants, when to sow vegetables, storing and freezing of fruit, the various types of shrubs, maintaining pools, caring for lawns, pruning, choosing equipment, and so on.

Like me, you may be ignorant about a lot of these things now. Don't worry, You're about to become an expert!

Chapter 1
Pot plants

Kind, if somewhat misguided, people are forever giving me pot plants. Misguided because I tend not to look after them very well, with the result that, more often than not, I have a death on my hands.

Where am I going wrong? Is it something to do with lack of water – or too much of it? Could it have something to do with natural gas central heating (commonly blamed nowadays by indoor gardeners I meet round the country whose Poinsettias are wilting or whose African Violets are failing to flower)?

Is there something in the 'green fingers' theory, or is that just a myth? Would talking to the plants help? (No, I'm not joking: I've met many gardeners who seriously believe that conversing with them really helps.)

Take the case of what was once an 'everbearing' Calamondin, or miniature orange tree, which was given to me after a *Nationwide* programme about indoor plants.

The tag around Calamondin's slim trunk informed me that she was 'the finest ornamental citrus known', which I found easy to believe.

The tiny oranges tasted rather tart, but they looked lovely as they grew in profusion: I was assured that one of the attractions of the plant was that it would bear fruit and blossom at the same time. And, from a practical point of view, the oranges would make delicious marmalade.

I never got that far. Within a few weeks of Calamondin (a native of the Philippine Islands) being entrusted to my care, the fruit began to look wrinkled and pathetic; the leaves became pale and brittle; and there was not a hint of blossom to be seen.

In a despairing effort to restore her to health and vigour, I re-read the instructions. 'Keep moist', they said, so I tried giving her more water. That only seemed to accelerate poor Calamondin's decline.

Would a foliar feed have helped? A bigger or a smaller pot, perhaps? Did she (if she was a she) require more sunlight?

If I learned anything from the sad demise of Calamondin, it was that you can't just stick a pot plant on the mantelpiece, water it regularly and hope for the best.

We took rather more care with the Poinsettia my wife was given for Christmas – a delightful plant with bright green leaves and red bracts which flourished in a moderately warm and bright room right through the winter and spring. It needed very little attention, which may be why we did so well with it!

Come June, fresh green foliage appeared while the bracts faded and fell. Time for action. But what precisely were we supposed to do?

A gardener whose advice I've learned to respect told me that I should throw the plant out and buy another one later in the year (God bless garden centres!). But that seemed too easy a way out. I wasn't going to learn anything that way, so I sought other advice.

'Cut it down to about 6 inches above the top of the pot', I was told. 'See that it has at least 12 hours of darkness every day through the winter. Take cuttings from the head of the plant.'

I don't know about you, but those kind of instructions don't satisfy me. I want to know WHY a plant should be cut down; what happens to the plant as a result; what effects daylight or darkness have; how a cutting develops roots, and so on.

Let's start at the beginning . . .

GAY NIGHTINGALE:
'Experiment with assorted plants'

Where does the interest in gardening come from in the first place? That's what I would like to know, Michael. Once the interest is there, anyone is well on the way to becoming an expert.

However, like you, I think there is still an awful lot to learn about plants. But isn't this, perhaps, the greatest reward that comes with gardening? An interest with infinite variation in form: there is always some new delight to be discovered.

But back to basics. You say your pot plants tend to die. If one or two plants do fade away, don't give up. Remember, even the most experienced gardeners suffer from the occasional specimen that doesn't do well. Either try again with the same kind of plant – you will probably have learned so much from your first mistakes that you will grow a flourishing plant at the second attempt – or try a different kind of plant.

For instance, take this problem of water. It's more than a question of too much or too little. This *is* important of course; and always err on the side of giving your houseplants slightly less than they need, rather than swamping them – you're likely to have less plants die that way.

You could feel the temperature of the water. Try to give tepid water to those plants which originate from warm countries. I'm not joking – you have to pamper plants if you want them to look nice in the home.

When watering, you should consider, too,

whether the plant is what we commonly call a 'lime hater' (many people think that plants can't 'like' or 'hate' anything, but we'll come to communications in a moment!)

If your plant is a 'lime hater' then it needs an acid or peaty compost, and alkaline tap-water won't do it much good. It is worth saving rain-water for special, expensive plants. Young plants can be re-potted in peaty compost at regular intervals. You'll find lime deposits leaking through small clay pots after any length of time on hard tap water.

Several enthusiasts claim that cold tea helps! I have tried it on busy lizzies with quite surprising effect. However, I would be wary of pouring it *ad lib* on precious plants. In any case, beware of unwanted tea-leaves. These should be composted in the garden before use.

Indoor gardeners are concerned about central heating. In my first house there was natural gas central heating, but dreadful draughty windows! The draught was directed at me not the plants, which had all the warmth they wanted and all the fresh air too!

So, I did notice the difference when we moved to a house with electric central heating and firmly closing windows – it was much less humid. But a moist atmosphere is what most houseplants need.

A humid atmosphere for plants can be easily provided by packing damp sphagnum moss or peat between pot and container. By maintaining this dampness with the addition of a little water each day, air around the plant will be kept moist.

An alternative is to use what is termed a 'plunge pot'. This can be a dish or tray containing water-bearing material in which the plant pot is stood – above the water level so that it does not take in excess moisture.

To keep the atmosphere humid around plants, they can be stood in containers that will hold moisture. Below: On stones which are covered with water or (above) the pot sunk into a larger pot with moist peat in the space between.

You mention particularly African Violets. These happen to be some of the plants that were growing on a south-facing window-sill with net curtains, which gave just the right amount of shade.

It took me some time to get used to growing them on a west-facing window-sill with no net curtains in my new house. The curtain *is* an important detail. You see, to gain flowers on your African Violets, they should be denied scorching sun, but certainly not kept too far from light.

Flowers appear on African Violets from May to December – with or without central heating – but it is more tricky during the other months without artificial light. Perhaps I can show you why plants are often described as needing shade and strong light.

Seeing African Violets growing in their native land was interesting. In Kenya, they are also raised in nurseries for the pot-plant market. But the big difference is that, whereas over here they are protected in glass houses, over there they are protected by large – as big as greenhouses – slatted wood structures. Thin slats – split bamboo – leave long cracks of light, which make stripey shadows on the benches.

It's obvious, when you are inside these structures with African gardeners, that what they call shade would be the same as our mildly sunny day, due to the difference in the intensity of light.

This is something to bear in mind when growing houseplants: many of them come from countries which are warm with bright sun all day. I suppose it does all come down to 'green fingers' in the end.

I think there is some truth in that saying. It's a kind of sympathy certain people have with plants. But I also believe that 'green fingers' would come to anybody who began to take an interest in plants. Is it linked to the 'talking to plants' idea, I wonder?

My earliest gardening memory as a little girl is walking round a walled mews cottage every morning before breakfast, beside a man who stopped at every plant and could be heard mumbling mathematics: 'Two xy squared over six to the power of three' or something similar.

He had an absent expression on his face; but he would be pulling out the odd weed, trying back the odd straggler, cutting back the odd creeper. The plants seemed to listen well to the mathematics!

I have also followed the progress of your Calamondin with curiosity. I wonder why you call it a 'she'?

The extra water would have 'accelerated poor Calamondin's decline' and so would a foliar feed at that juncture. Feeding of any kind is always reserved for healthy, fast-growing plants, often during the long summer months only. The same applies to potting-on. A plant that is obviously top-heavy usually needs a slightly larger container; try to get a pot one size bigger, rather than twice the size, and go up in stages as the plant grows. That is a fairly general rule.

But I have to mention that there are always exceptions to rules – some plants rest in summer for example – but mostly it's the other way round.

The sun would have helped. Shall we attempt to get the miniature orange growing instructions straight? Regarding water, you want to give plenty in summer, when the plant is making new growth. Give diluted liquid fertiliser every two weeks from the beginning of March until October. For the rest of the year allow the soil to dry between waterings.

Full sunlight is necessary – in terms of houseplants this means your sunniest win-

Re-potting is generally done in the spring or early summer, never in winter. First, tap the plant out carefully; examine to see if the roots are filling the existing pot; select a pot which is not more than 2 inches greater in top diameter; set to correct depth, generally about half-an-inch deeper than before. Leave space for watering.

dow will be best. In winter, the temperature of the room shouldn't fall below 50° F. A living-room is sometimes too dry if the heat is left on for most of the day. Often a bedroom is better with its odd hours of heating – just to keep the room from getting too cold.

You can prune citrus plants into pretty round ball shapes on short tree trunks. Then even the foliage is attractive, as it is ever-green.

Why do we prune pot plants? Partly for shape, tidiness, and keeping the specimen to the size we want it; partly to stimulate growth from below the cut-line. On a citrus plant, you make lots of young stems and light green leaves appear, contrasting with the darker green, leathery old leaves.

It isn't a bad idea to get your hand in by growing some ordinary orange pips. This gives you practice, and you might be lucky enough to produce flowers.

But why do we take cuttings of Cala-mondin, rather than grow it cheaply from pips? Here is a fundamental question. Almost all gardening is based on this principle: if we sow seeds we get variety; if we take cuttings or offsets we get the same as the plant in hand. Therefore, orange pips will produce a mixed batch of plants – some will flower young, some won't. If we take cuttings of Calamondin, for example, we are sure there will be flowers within a couple of years or so.

And so it goes on: we sow seeds until we produce something exciting, then we take cuttings of the plant we like in order to gain more examples of the specimen. It can be more complicated with genes and F1 hybrids, but unless you are going in for pot plants in a big way it doesn't matter whether you know this or not.

In other houseplants, as well as the oranges, mostly stem cuttings are used, that is short side-shoots with a few leaves. They will often root if poked into compost and placed on a sunny window-sill. Try it.

But African Violets are amusing. You can take a single leaf. Merely rest a large leaf on a small jar with the stalk just reaching into water. If you watch for two or three weeks, you'll see roots emerge from the cut end of the stalk. Later little leaves appear around these roots, and you will have the beginnings of more than one new plant.

In the home, this can be done over a warm radiator shelf (or similar) in winter; or on a sun-warmed window-sill in summer – with some shade.

You ask about your poinsettia. I think you did well with it. You had months of colour, which – as far as I can see – is the only reason for having these plants indoors. I wouldn't throw a healthy pot plant away. Keep your poinsettia for another year, is my advice. Put it in a warmish place on your lightest window-sill.

In winter, give enough water to maintain crisp leaves and bracts. Too little water will cause them to drop early. Give lukewarm water when the compost seems to be going dry; but never leave the pot in water, or have visible water on top of the compost after a few seconds.

Start to use diluted fertiliser from the end of April, or re-pot into fresh compost. Plants *are* usually pruned back to six inches – for reasons already explained. And this is done at re-potting time.

Commercially, cuttings are taken from the new shoots, which root easily enough if you give them bottom heat – warm soil. In fact in Kenya, where these plants with bright red bracts are to be seen all year, people cut poin-settia as a weed and throw cuttings to one side. Cut ends form roots naturally with no attention.

The reason poinsettias are in flower every month in Africa (actually they came from Mexico originally) is due to the almost equal length of day and night all year.

So it follows that, when the long days begin to shorten in England, buds begin to form naturally in poinsettias. There are ways of putting plants in the dark for part of the day to gain the same effect. But in the home it is easy to wait until the short day causes the bracts to appear some time during the winter. It is as simple as that.

I hope you'll keep your plant.

Chapter 2
Lawns

What does the word 'turf' mean to you?

When I was a lad, it could have only one meaning. It was usually preceded by the word 'sacred' – and the most sacred turf of all was a rectangular greenish-brown patch, 22 yards long, in the middle of Yorkshire Cricket Club's ground at Headingley, Leeds.

Nowadays, I'm more inclined to think of turf as rolling fairways or velvet-like greens on a golf course. To others, I suppose, The Turf is something on which racehorses run away with their shirts.

Gardeners, naturally, think of the turf as their lawn – as like as not, the centre-piece of their garden and (if postcards to *Gardeners' Question Time* are anything to go by) the thing that gives them most problems.

There are two kinds of lawn. There's the one we all want – green, lush, flatter than a pancake, bereft of weeds or disease, unmarked by incontinent dogs or cats, unspoiled by worms or busy badgers.

Then there's the one we nearly all have – a botanical experience – a showpiece of clover, moss, daisies, buttercups, Yorkshire fog, dandelions and just about every variety of grass known to man. Like mine, in fact.

I've always regarded the first kind as unattainable and the second as quite attractive provided it's regularly mown and the edges kept trim, but I'm prepared to aim for higher things if somebody would tell me how.

Mind you, during 1973 with its long, dry spring and summer, keeping even the most variegated lawn healthy was a formidable task. As the Fisons people said in their Press hand-out which they optimistically send me each month, 'the lawn is always a problem in dry weather'. They could say that again.

They went on: 'There is no doubt that to keep all grass fresh and green all the time, water has to be applied, and in greater quantities than most of us realise. But much can be done by giving the right treatment in the winter and spring. Lawns regularly spiked all over, and with peat brushed into the holes, will suffer far less from drought because when watered, or when rain falls, it is held like a sponge and the roots can take advantage of it.'

That's the story of my gardening life: when I have a problem in the summer, there's always someone around to tell me what I should have done in the winter and spring.

During June, for my *Garden News* column, I went in search of advice on coping with what by then were drought conditions, and I called on Roger Taylor at the ICI research station at Jealotts Hill in Berkshire.

He told me that, after a fortnight or so without rain, it's important to start watering before the lawn becomes too dry. Applying solid or liquid nitrogen fertiliser at the same time will help and it seems likely that the liquid will bring the quicker response, though there's only slight concrete evidence of this.

Most people still cut the grass too short in dry spells of weather. Don't. It takes the growing heart away and can be very harmful.

When you do mow the lawn, be sure to rake off the cuttings if you're not using a box. There's a widespread belief that leaving the cuttings will keep the lawn damp, but that's a fallacy. All they do is to prevent light rain getting through to the turf.

Old-established lawns bring the biggest problems in dry weather. They tend to have a high proportion of annual grass (Poa annua) which produces seed and dies if it's starved of water.

Roger added some useful tips for reseeding an old lawn that's infested with weeds. Here's how:

Apply a selective weedkiller. Do nothing after that for six weeks, then treat the lawn with a paraquat-based weedkiller.

Wait another fortnight, then mow as closely as possible. Rake, taking off the dead material and scratching up the ground.

Apply a general fertiliser – two ounces to the square yard – and a light top dressing of soil, peat or a mixture of the two.

Sprinkle on seed . . . and three weeks later you have a lovely new lawn, without having had to dig up the old one.

It all sounds so simple, but how do I keep the darned thing that way?

How long will it be before patches of pearlwort appear? How should I counter the drips from overhanging trees turning my nice new grass into a sort of black slime – or the incursion of countless weeds from the open fields which surround my garden?

Cat's ear, bird's foot trefoil, sheep's sorrel, mouse-ear chickweed, speed-well, parsley piert, self-heal, crowfoot, hawkbit . . . they're all lovely names, and in their way lovely flowers, but how do I keep them out of my patch – especially if they're rampant in my neighbour's?

As for the coarse grasses, which are decidedly unlovely, I'm told there's no chemical method of controlling them. So what's to be done?

(I still have to be convinced, incidentally, that there's any better method, anywhere in the garden, than weeding by hand. I really don't see the point of applying chemicals which simply turn green weeds into yellow ones.)

From time to time, modern research produces developments which seem tailor-made for people like me who have little time and less skill available for labouring in the garden.

My friend Fred Loads, for instance, has spent years perfecting a new kind of turf that comes ready-made in rolls and can be laid just like a carpet. That kind of thing sounds just the job for me.

But, once laid, it will still need cutting. And weeding. And watering. And feeding.

I have a nasty feeling that there's no short cut to the perfect lawn. And no substitute for hard labour . . .

PETER PESKETT:
'No magic wand for lawns'

Stop dreaming the impossible dream, Michael. That lush, green sward you regard as unattainable *can* become a reality if you'll wake up to the fact that lawns, like plants, need lavish love, care and attention if they're to look their best. If you're not prepared to give your lawn the time and devotion it deserves, then you've only got yourself to blame if it gradually degenerates into a cross between an end-of-season soccer pitch and a wild, unkempt meadow.

And there is no magic horticultural wand you can wave over a second-rate lawn to turn it into a spread of bowling-green perfection. No, like the perfect child, the first-class lawn has to be nurtured properly right from the start, for no amount of corrective therapy along the way will wipe out any major initial errors made in raising it from tiny seed to healthy, pleasing maturity.

Of course, some gardeners deliberately opt for a lawn of inferior quality. These are usually parents of young, active kids, and they realise at the outset that it would be a complete waste of time, money and expertise to create a super lawn only to see it ruined by their lively offspring.

So, at the planning stage, the first important task is to decide exactly what sort of lawn you want. A utility lawn because you know it will have a fair amount of traffic over it? Or a luxury lawn, a showpiece of close-cut perfection which will be strictly out-of-bounds to marauding youngsters? You *have* to make the choice, for there are different sorts of grasses ideal for one or the other.

Naturally, the utility lawn should be composed of grasses which are broad-leaved and tough enough to withstand hard wear. Rough-stalked meadow grass (Poa trivialis), Smooth-stalked meadow grass (Poa pratensis), Creeping red fescue (Festuca rubra genuina), Chewings fescue (Festuca rubra fallax), Crested dog's-tail (Cynosurus cristatus) and Perennial ryegrass (Lolium perenne) fall into this category. Indeed, these grasses are the ones most commonly found in utility lawn seed mixtures and are ideal for all soils apart from very heavy clays. This type of soil is cold and unsuitable for fescues, so these should be replaced in the mixture by Timothy (Phleum pratense), which does very well on clay.

For a luxury lawn, fine-leaved grasses such as Creeping bent (Agrostis stolonifera), Browntop bent (Agrostis tenuis) and Velvet bent (Agrostis canina) should be used. A typical standard proprietary mixture consists of 60% Chewings fescue, 20% Creeping red fescue and 20% Browntop bent, though super-quality mixes omit Creeping red fescue altogether, with the proportion of Chewings fescue going up to 80%. Chewings fescue has dark-green leaves which keep their colour well throughout the year, and it is very resistant to dry soil conditions. Browntop bent also stands up well to dry weather and, although it is fine-leaved, it has a tough blade.

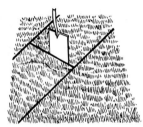

Repair bumps in a lawn by first cutting an 'H' shape over the bump with a spade; folding back the turf and removing excess soil; and then replacing the turf.

Fill a hollow in the lawn by cutting squares of turf from around the hollow and filling in with top soil, levelling off, and then returfing.

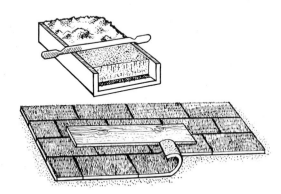

A mechanical spreader guarantees uniform broadcasting of both lawn seed and fertilisers.

Make sure every turf is the same thickness by placing each one grass-side down in a box, the sides of which are exactly as deep as the turf should be, and then add or remove soil as necessary. Then lay the turves in a 'brick wall' pattern, standing on a plank to spread the pressure.

Two further grasses are ideal for shady situations. Wood meadow grass (Poa nemoralis), a medium-textured grass, flourishes in shady, damp conditions and is ideal for growing under trees, and Wavy-hair grass (Deschampsia flexuosa) thrives in sunless, sandy conditions.

Having chosen a suitable grass mixture, the next task is to decide on the positioning, size and shape of the lawn. In an ornamental garden, an area as near as possible to the rear of the house is by far the best position, because the lawn, and all the other features which make up the garden, should be looked upon as an extension of the home, with the lawn being the carpet of this 'outdoor room'. It is silly to hide the lawn behind a bank of trees and shrubs so that it cannot be seen from the house; though this may be wholly desirable if it is designed purely and simply as a playground for the kids!

When it comes to size, there is one major pitfall to avoid. Many gardeners faced with creating a small garden from scratch fill a comparatively large area of their site with a lawn, only to find later that there is not enough room left for the other garden features they would have liked to incorporate. So on a small plot, think small – remembering that a garden completely dominated by grass looks as incomplete as a garden with no lawn at all.

As for shape, most gardens tend to be longer than they are wide, so it makes sense that a lawn should be shaped in the same way – roughly rectangular. But avoid straight lines wherever possible. A lawn with curved sides and rounded corners can make all the difference between a boring, dull overall effect and one of immense interest and character. Further interest and beauty can be added by planting trees, ornamental or fruit, in the lawn, and I think there are few gardening sights more delightful than spring bulbs growing in the grass of a lawn.

Moving on to planting, there are, of course, two ways of creating a lawn: by sowing or turfing . . . and you *must* sow for a top quality lawn. The single big advantage of turf is that it gives an 'instant garden', but it is difficult to get hold of turf made up of good quality grasses. So I only advise using the turfing method if you're after a second-rate, utility lawn.

If you decide on the turfing method, shop around for 'parkland' turf, which consists of reasonably good grasses with some of the coarser species, or Cumberland sea-washed turf, which is made solely of fine-bladed, dwarf-growing grasses and is very expensive. Also, it is only suitable for laying on light to medium soils.

Turf laying is best carried out in the autumn. The site should be level or evenly sloped and, one week before laying, a well-balanced proprietary lawn food should be scattered over the ground at 2 oz per square metre. When ordering turf, make sure it will be delivered in manageable strips, preferably in lengths of one metre with a width of 30 centimetres and a depth of about 4 centimetres. Before putting each turf in place, check its thickness by placing it, grass-side downwards, in a suitable size wooden box, slightly larger than the required turf area and about 4 centimetres deep, slicing off any turf which protrudes above the box with an edging iron or old carving knife.

When laying, start at one end of the site and work forward, with your feet standing on the turves already laid. It is wise to stand on a long plank over the newly-laid turves to prevent them being damaged by uneven foot pressure. Lay one line of turves end to end (removing any weeds from them as you go along) and firm each one in by hand. Should there be any depressions, lift the turf and place some fresh soil underneath until it is at the correct level. Next, lay the second row of turves so they alternate with the first, in the same way as a builder lays bricks. Then carry on laying the turves in the same pattern over the whole area.

When laying is finished, the edges will be irregular and the lawn should now be trimmed into the final shape you have planned. Lay a long piece of string or rope on the grass in the required shape and cut along its edge with an edging iron, with the blade sloping slightly outwards to give the lawn an angled edge, which is stronger than a vertical one. To finish the job, brush sand or fine soil into the cracks between the turves to knit them together quickly.

A lawn laid from turf needs about a month to settle down. During this time it should be watered if there is a distinct lack of rain and rolled lightly if any very uneven patches appear. After the four weeks are up, give the lawn its first cut, with the mower blades set moderately high at about 2 centimetres. Then follow this cut with another light rolling if any unevenness persists.

The best months for sowing a lawn are between August and early October, and from April to early May, with autumn being the ideal time, so that the site can be dug, levelled and prepared the previous winter and spring and left grassless over summer. By doing this, any weeds which appear can be hoed off or forked out before they have a chance to establish or re-seed themselves on the site. The ground will be clear of weeds by the autumn and the grass seed will germinate readily and grow without competition from weeds. The grass will then establish a good root system over the winter and be ready to sustain rapid leaf growth in spring.

When you buy your seed the supplier will advise in what quantities to sow, though it is wise to add 25% to his figures to allow for the depredations of birds! The most common way of broadcasting seed is, of course, by hand, but many people are finding a wheeled fertiliser distributor handy for this job because it guarantees uniform spreading. After sowing, rake the ground over to protect most of the seeds from birds, and firm it to bring the seed into close contact with the soil and so assist the germination process. As the grass germinates, any bare patches which show up should be re-seeded immediately. Finally, use shears to cut a newly-sown lawn until it becomes fully established, and so prevent pulling the grass up by its roots.

By sowing properly – or by laying top quality turf – you're well on the way to obtaining Michael Barratt's 'unattainable' luxury lawn. But it won't stay at the peak of perfec-

tion unless you lavish it with loving care and protection. It will need feeding, mowing, watering, weeding and repairing . . . neglect any one of these major jobs and you get the problems Michael's landed himself with.

A lawn needs food to survive. Not a horticultural feast, but sufficient nutrients to enable each grass root to produce fresh top growth every day through spring and summer. The nutrients grass needs are nitrogen, phosphates, potash (containing potassium), calcium, magnesium, iron, manganese, copper and boron, and all these are found in the various excellent proprietary lawn foods. Most of these foods can be used at intervals throughout the season, always following the supplier's instructions, though it is worth bearing in mind that a fertiliser applied in spring should be rich in nitrogen to encourage green growth, and in the autumn high in phosphate and potash to persuade roots to flourish.

But the most important part of the feeding process is the actual application of the fertiliser. If it's not broadcast evenly, the lawn can finish up looking like a chess board with burnt, brown patches where the dressing has been over-applied. So it's wise to invest in a wheeled fertiliser distributor (which, as I have pointed out, will also be a help when sowing the lawn) to ensure uniform application. Take

After turves have been laid, brush sand, fine soil or peat over the grass and into the cracks between turves to knit them together quickly.

care not to apply the food in dry weather, otherwise the whole lawn may become scorched and brown. If no rain falls for 48 hours after you've applied the fertiliser, give the lawn a good watering.

And this brings us to watering generally. Moisture is essential to all plants, and grass is no exception. Also, on lawns, any fertilisers applied can only be put to good use when they are taken down into the soil by rain to form soluble salts. But a lawn should only be watered when it starts to show signs of a shortage of moisture. There is a marked reduction in the rate of growth of a thirsty lawn and there will be a yellowing or light brown discolouration of the grasses. Another point to watch is that lawns growing on sandy soils, which drain rapidly, suffer from a lack of water much sooner than those on loams, which retain moisture more readily. And a sloping lawn will lose moisture from its higher levels faster than from its lower levels.

The best time of the day to water is in the evening, when the temperature falls and evaporation of mositure from the lawn slows. Always apply planty of water, but be careful not to overdo it: if pools begin to appear, stop watering immediately. If the lawn becomes waterlogged, the grass will die because air cannot get to its roots. Finally, always water a newly-sown lawn with a fine sprinkler to avoid disturbing the roots.

Now on to that most energetic of jobs – mowing. Dealing first with newly-sown lawns, these should be given their first cut when the grass is about 3 centimetres in height, with the mower blades set so that they will cut the lawn 2 centimetres above ground level. Mature lawns should be mown for the first time in late March or early April, again with the blades set to give a 2-centimetre cut. Over the next few weeks, the height of the cut should be lowered, but never to less than 1 centimetre.

Ideally, a lawn should be mowed at least once a week during the summer, except during a drought when the growth rate is substantially reduced and it is wise to leave a thicker coat of grass to reduce the rate of water loss from the soil surface.

Weeds are a problem on most lawns, but positive steps can be taken to control them. Daisies and plantains can be controlled by applying lawn sand, though this treatment will not deter more persistent aliens such as chickweed, ribwort and clover. These should be treated with selective, hormone weed-killers, which can be applied either as a liquid or as a dry mixture with fertiliser. But remember . . . don't mow the lawn for three days before and after weedkiller has been applied; don't use the mowings for mulching until the lawn has been mown four times after application; don't use composted mowings for at least six months; don't apply weedkiller to newly-sown grass or new turf.

Finally, a few hints on general care, maintenance and repairing. Aerate your lawn regularly with a garden fork. Brush with a besom (or witch's) broom to fluff up the grass. Get rid of fungal diseases by applying a proprietary fungicide. Brush the lawn to get rid of worm casts and ant hills; remove mole hills with a spade. Repair any depressions by cutting the turf, folding it back and adding extra soil underneath. Repair bumps the same way, removing soil instead. Use a rake or broom to get rid of autumn leaves, which can kill the grass if they are not cleared. Rake before mowing to make both grass and creeping weeds stand erect ready for cutting.

And just one last word on those incontinent dogs and cats Michael Barratt seems to have trouble with. If you're around when they're 'spending a penny', dilute the urine immediately with a liberal sprinkling of water to reduce the risk of patches of grass being killed.

Chapter 3
Equipment

If you think that gardening is back-breaking work, you haven't read any good advertisements lately.

According to our more with-it manufacturers, modern gardening consists of nothing more strenuous than placing a scantily clad blonde beauty on the padded seat of an all-pupose mechanical cultivator, sitting back in your deck chair and gazing into her eyes, or whatever else it is that turns you on, and watching your garden grow while the machine does all the work.

Strangely, that hasn't been my experience.

I've told the story before of how I acquired a garden along with an Elizabethan house some years ago in the Staffordshire hamlet of Stretton near the village of Brewood, and of how I learned that there's no easy way out when it comes to turning a patch of land into a thing of beauty.

This 'garden' was half an acre of ground which looked as though it hadn't been cultivated since the original owner went off to meet the Armada with Drake.

When we moved in, I contemplated this wasteland with some despair and eventually decided that the only way to make a start was with a scythe. So I ambled up the road (everything in that isolated corner of England was done at less than walking pace) to introduce myself to our neigbouring farmer.

He clearly regarded me as a foreigner, a city slicker in my collar and tie. His name was Archie and he immediately launched into a lecture on the need to conform to the well-preserved ways of the local folk, and especially to be respectful to the local landowner.

'God bless the squire and his relations,' he quoted at me, 'and keep us in our proper stations.' It was like stepping back a century or more in time.

Cagily, I broached the subject of a scythe and the possibility of borrowing his.

He looked me up and down in disbelief. 'Do you know how to handle a scythe? Have you learned how to keep it sharp?'

I was out of my depth and confessed it. Well, as an alternative, a friend had suggested I might buy some geese. They'd soon eat through all that long grass, wouldn't they?

'Geese? Geese!' He was incredulous. 'They mess all over the place. You'd be ankle deep in muck in no time at all.'

Oh, well, how about a couple of goats?

That was the last straw. 'What would you do with a goat in kid? Do you know how to milk one? What do you do for a living, anyway?'

I raised myself to full height and told him proudly:

'I'm a television commentator.'

Sheer disgust written all over his face, he raised his ancient cap, threw it on the ground, and exclaimed: 'Holy Mary!'.

Later, Archie and I became friends and he kindly brought his tractor down to plough up our 'garden'. It was a start, but no more, and in the ensuing years I learned a thing or two about garden equipment by making plenty of mistakes and spending a lot of money.

The altercation about the scythe, of course, had been my first lesson: no tool, however simple or however sophisticated, is the slightest use if you don't know how to use it.

I know now that even something as basic as a spade needs the most careful selection. For a start, it has to be properly balanced (though I still haven't learned how to make sure that the balance is right for me). Digging is never really easy work, but I'm sure we often make it a darned sight harder than it need be by using too large a blade, or handling the thing in a way guaranteed to do ourselves a spinal injury in no time at all.

Stainless steel tools, in my experience, make the actual work lighter because there's no corrosion with the result that friction is reduced to a minimum.

But stainless steel has one basic snag – it's considerably more expensive. I suppose, when all's said and done, that you get what you pay for. That's an old cliché, but I have an important variation on it: I never pay the full price for what I get.

Neither manufacturers nor retailers of garden equipment will like my saying this, but there's one sure way of paying a little less for your tools. Bargain with the shopkeeper.

My usual ploy is to ask: 'How much for cash?'. You can be confident of lopping five or even ten per cent off the list price. That way, you may be able to afford tools that will last a lifetime rather than cheaper ones that will have to be replaced every few years.

But there are still many questions to which I don't know the answers.

Should I use a Dutch or a draw hoe – or one of those new-fangled shapes that seem to be multiplying like golf putters?

What are the best for my large lawn – cylinder or rotary mowers?

Sometimes I'm appalled at my ignorance!

GEOFF WRIGHT:
'Quality pays in the long run'

Let's face it, gardening can be hard work, but given the right tools for the job our task can be made easier – and the 'end-product' is bound to be better.

First of all don't overburden yourself with too many implements, but go for quality; it pays in the long run.

Well, basically, what do you need? A spade, fork, rake, Dutch and draw hoes, trowel, hand fork, secateurs, shears – and, of course, a lawnmower.

Nearly all of us have a lawn, so let's start with mowers. There are two ways to cut grass – by revolving cylinder, or by rotary action. Rotaries have become popular in recent years, because they are capable of cutting long, 'problem' grass, and are also effective on short lawn grass. With a cylinder machine you can only cut lawn grass. So it depends really on your particular garden.

If you only have a lawn, go for a cylinder mower. It can't be beaten for fine cutting. If you also have to cope with tall grass on verges and other difficult places, buy a rotary. One other point to remember is that, with a few exceptions, rotaries do not collect the grass whereas cylinder mowers do.

Now, what about driving power? You can choose just man-power if you are energetic or, for an easier life, a motor mower, or a mains or battery electric. There's one thing about electric mowers, you get silent operation. But some people dislike dragging an electric cable about, and this can also be a problem if you are a long way from a power point. You can, however, overcome this with a battery model which is self-contained and runs off a car-type battery.

Always clean your mower after you have finished. You don't want to be faced next time with a grass-clogged machine.

In the average garden there's no way to avoid digging, so let's discuss spades and forks. These really are the basics of cultivation and either can be used for turning over the soil.

When the going is hard, a fork is best. It's easier to push in than a spade, and when you are digging up large clods of earth you can break them up by giving the clods a sharp clout with the back of the fork.

Stainless steel, though expensive, is undoubtedly the best. There's no rusting and the implements slide into the soil with the minimum of effort.

Don't forget that there are different sizes, and some manufacturers make a wide range, but really we need only bother about two – the full-sized standard spade or fork, and the so-called border version. Incidentally, some manufacturers make junior-sized tools as well, so you can start the kids off early in life!

The smaller, border-sized tools were designed for women, but the ease with which they can be handled has made them popular with everyone. If you only have a fairly small plot the border type can be recommended.

When you buy, pick up the tool and test its weight. If it is very heavy you'll soon tire yourself out when it comes to using it. Weight doesn't necessarily mean strength. You can get strength and lightness.

Be careful, also, to see (and this applies to all implements) that the handle is strongly fixed into its socket. And don't forget the handle itself, which should be the right length, strength and smoothness. In addition to wood some are now made of polypropylene which is durable and weather resistant. There are 'T' and 'D' topped handles – it's just a matter of which suits you best.

We've dug it, so now let's rake it. There is not a lot to say about the rake, except that it is probably the most used and the most versatile of all garden tools.

So many jobs can be done with it: breaking up the soil, levelling, working in fertilisers, even pulling out weeds. A handle of the right length, and strength in the teeth are the main essentials. The 12-toothed type is suitable for everyday use, but there are some wider heads with more teeth. The more teeth there are, the finer the raked area will be.

Also very useful is the fan-shaped wire rake for removing cut grass, leaves and other debris.

There are a number of different types of hoe, but for our purposes two basic styles can be considered. First the Dutch hoe with a D-shaped or flat-bladed head, for breaking up the soil surface, and the draw hoe for earthing up, or drawing up the soil round plants. It is also used for making seed drills (grooves in the earth) when sowing. The gardener really needs both types of hoe.

A hand trowel and hand fork are essential and, again, the old familiar kinds are best. Smooth handled and preferably stainless steel, they are needed for planting out, weeding, and a multitude of jobs. Some very small, almost toy-sized, trowels are available and are useful for houseplants.

You'll need a pair of secateurs for pruning. Advice here is simple: just buy a good quality pair (they are not expensive). Look for hard-wearing, sharp blades, easy action, comfortable handles, and lightness.

You will probably have a hedge of some kind, often all-important if you want a little privacy in these days of close-packed houses – so shears are next on the list.

Here is a case when cheapness is bound to be false economy. There is no argument – a top quality pair pays off. Go for lightness, as this can make all the difference both to the finish of the hedge and the strain on your arms. Comfortable handles, too, are vital. Good, smooth, wooden ones are perhaps the best. Metal handles add to the weight, and some with rubber or plastic grips are not always satisfactory, especially in hot weather.

Shears, of course, are used for other things besides hedge trimming. Edging lawns, for instance, and here, although short-handled types can be used, a pair of long-handled edging shears with blades at right-angles to the handles save bending and take the backache out of this job.

A few words about pots might be helpful. There is the traditional clay in a wide range of sizes from a top width of 2 inches upwards. Incidentally, new clay pots should be soaked in water for a few hours before being used. An

advantage of these pots is that they are porous, enabling the plant to breathe, but moisture is absorbed by the pots, and soil in them dries out quicker, so you will have to add water more often than with less porous kinds.

Plastic pots are now widely used and are light in weight, easy to clean, break less easily and therefore last longer than clay. As they retain moisture, the danger of overwatering must be watched.

The ambitious gardener will also aim at owning a greenhouse, and this is dealt with in a separate chapter.

One can spend a fortune on garden tools these days. Manufacturers seem to provide a never-ending supply of new ideas but, to start off with, the equipment mentioned in this chapter should 'fill the bill'. Many things grow on trees – but not money, unfortunately.

The handles of tools are largely a matter of personal choice. When buying a spade, try it first to find out what suits you best. These two alternatives are generally available.

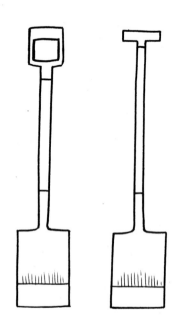

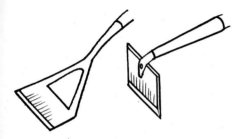

These two types of hoe are for specific purposes. The one on the left is a dutch hoe used walking backwards so that the ground is not re-trodden. Generally for small weeds between rows. Shown right is a drag hoe used between bigger crops and for bigger weeds.

The two main types of mowers are the rotary bladed and the conventional cutting cylinder. The rotary will cut grass of different lengths and is particularly good for orchards, etc. The cylinder type will cut shorter and is generally considered to make a better job of a decorative lawn. Some rotary mowers have attachments for gathering the grass, while cylinder mowers can be used with or without the grass box.

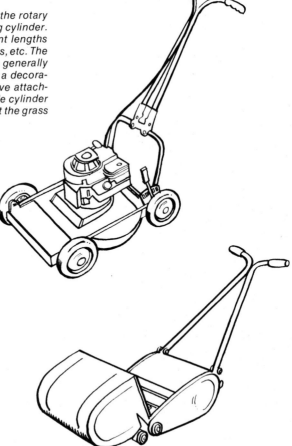

Chapter 4
Composts & fertilisers

'Come now, Johnny, eat up your porridge or you won't grow up to be a big strong man like your father.'

The admonitions of parents make sense, even if we didn't think so when we were children. The body needs proper nutrients if it is to develop healthily.

When I was a lad, it was drummed into me that a balanced diet was essential for my future physical welfare. If I didn't drink enough milk each day, my teeth would surely fall out through lack of calcium. If I didn't eat plenty of carrots, with their high vitamin C content, how could I expect to see in the dark? (My formative years were during the war, you understand.)

Joking apart, some parental brainwashing on how the human body grows gave me a fundamental understanding about the needs of plants. It was easier to appreciate that they needed nitrogen for growth and greenery; phosphate to develop their root systems, and potassium to encourage flowers and fruit.

Then doubts began. In human terms, the medical profession started to come up with a whole new series of theories about the value of what had been essential foods.

Milk? It might keep your teeth in place – but be careful, old chap, because it has a high cholesterol content and could lead to a heart condition.

Carrots? A waste of time unless you eat them raw, because cooking robs them of the health-giving vitamins.

Dieting became a national fad and a kind of mass hypochondria set in, certainly questioning all the old-established ideas about our bodies' needs and encouraging a whole new range of patented pills and potions.

Much the same happened in the garden. Learned articles were written about the possibly deleterious effects of overdoing this or that simple fertiliser. 'Soil additives' were developed with complex formulae – and fancy labels. Fertilisers became 'compound' and a great deal of money was spent on promoting their wondrous properties.

I'm frankly dubious about some of the new cultural cure-alls on the market. But is that because I'm an old fuddy-duddy, burying my head in the inorganic sand?

And another thing: how am I supposed to make a good compost?

Some of my respected friends in the gardening world tell me that anything which once lived can be usefully piled on the compost heap. But does that include old boots (once part of an animal) and back numbers of *Garden News* (which began life as a tree)?

Others tell me that I should be much more selective, that I should carefully avoid putting diseased plants, or tough weeds like ground elder, or woody material on my heap – and that I should add a proprietary brand of 'activator'.

I once had a comfortable belief in the natural properties of farmyard manure, believing that it provided not only vital nutrients for plant growth but also better soil texture. Now I'm told that it can make the soil sour, unless I add lime as a neutraliser.

True or false? Does it depend on the kind of manure – or the kind of soil? Anyway, how am I to determine what kind of soil there is in my garden? It's no use my taking a fancy in a nurseryman's catalogue to some plant that is described, say, as 'lime-loving' if I have no means of knowing whether my soil is acid or alkaline.

Once I have established the deficiencies, should I treat with organic or inorganic, solid or liquid fertilisers?

I'm hungry and thirsty for knowledge.

GEOFF AMOS:
'The earth is on the gardener's side'

The gardener in doubt about his own, or his garden's ability to grow a crop, need only look around him to see that the ground can hardly be prevented from supporting life. Trees and bushes, and the things we call weeds, abound and thrive with no help at all from a spade, a bag of fertiliser or an ounce of sweat.

True it is that some soils will grow things better than others. True also that certain plants don't take kindly to ingredients in particular types of soil, but the basic require-ments for growth are there in anything that can possibly be called soil. The earth is on the gardener's side everywhere.

But nature's way of gardening is different to ours. She doesn't try to grow things that aren't in their natural places, as we do. She doesn't expect plants from the Equator and near the North Pole to exist side by side in the same few square yards, as we do. She doesn't crave for things out of season, nor harvest and carry off masses of leaves, stems and roots, and expect others to grow in the same place in a few short months.

But, in accord with the scale of space and time with which she works, she cultivates the ground and adds all the richness and fertilisers necessary. She provides all the minerals and minute traces of things that plants need from the rocks of the earth. From the natural order of animals and plants living and dying, comes a wealth of fertility. And the cultivation, such as is necessary, is done by the wind and weather, and the mass of life the soil contains.

The new gardener need not think, then, that everything depends on him, and that if he doesn't know exactly what is in his soil his whole garden will fail completely. Whatever soil he has will contain the basic essentials for growth.

But, because he is looking for super growth, he must do his best to ensure super conditions. Nature's way, slightly exaggerated, is all he needs to create a super garden.

His first task then, must be to find out at what level he is starting. It helps to know the history of the place. Is it made-up ground for instance? Pushed from kingdom come by a bulldozer perhaps? If so it can be anything from the precious top-soil of what was once someone's beloved allotment, to the near barren sub-soil from feet under some concrete foundations somewhere. And if it's the latter, he's not only got his own work to do,

but he's got to catch up with what nature hasn't been able to do for a few hundred years perhaps. Either that or he'll have to bury it again with some imported top soil.

If it is the natural soil of the place, does the ground all around produce healthy specimens? Is it the country for apples, or cabbages, or rhododendrons and heathers? Does anyone nearby make his living by growing plants and, if so, what? Professional people don't struggle as a rule trying to make things grow in places where they won't.

What doesn't matter anywhere near as much as most beginners think is whether the ground is heavy or light. What the experienced gardener rates as ideal, and calls a good strong loam – basically clay, tempered with root fibre and sand – is generally looked on with horror by the newcomer anyway, who tends to think that soil should break up and run like sand.

What matters most about the nature of soils is their capacity to hold or to get rid of water. Water is the key that unlocks all doors. The ideal for all plants, except the extremes of desert or bog species, is for them to have access to water at all times, without having to be stood in it. It's like keeping a man happy by putting a glass of beer where he can always reach it, but not sickening him by making him stand up to his neck in it.

Although it is the heavy clay soils that are most likely to drown plants, even light soils

Good farmyard manure contains everything the garden needs – humus, fertilisers and trace elements.

The compost heap should be rather more than a heap of rubbish. Special containers can be bought, or made from wire netting. In any case air must not be excluded. It is important to have layers of materials of different textures, ie, lawn mowings, hedge clippings, cabbage leaves, kitchen waste.

can be bogs. It depends on the conditions underneath. Clay soils may be well drained. Light soils may be on top of clay and have a high water table. Either of these conditions will make an ideal garden, yet they look totally different on the top. The heavy soil will naturally hold water, yet the surplus will drain away. The light soil will absorb moisture by capillary action from the water lying underneath.

What we are most likely to find is either a soil that is sticky in winter and bakes hard in the summer, or one that can be dug and walked on even when wet, but that dries to a powder and will almost blow away in the wind. Lucky is the man with something just in between.

The material that will bring these two extremes nearer together is humus, the name given to nature's rotting waste materials. Dug in, it will loose moisture through the clay, hold it in the sand, open up the heavy ground, bind together the light. The form it is in hardly matters, as long as it is decomposing. It is the 'muck' part of the expert's 'muck and magic' formula. And because farmyard manure contains both these ingredients, it is by far the best form to use.

But the 'magic' can be bought in a packet, a bottle or a polythene bag these days, so any 'muck' – or let's go back to being polite and call it humus – will do. Leaves and leaf mould, peat, spent hops, seaweed and old mushroom compost are fair examples of it, ready for use as they are. Straw, garden and kitchen waste, and yes, old boots and newspapers – though I should have thought *Garden News* would have been more use on the bookshelf – must go on the compost heap first, because the rotting-down process takes energy from the soil when such materials as these are dug straight in.

But there are rules for a compost heap if it is to be efficient. Make it no less than five feet square at the base, and build it so that it tapers off slightly towards the top. Keep it loose to let the air in. Never use too much of one material at a time. Too many lawn mowings, for instance, will go sour. Don't put in diseased plants, for safety's sake. Don't expect bindweed, ground elder or dandelions to die just because they are out of sight for a few weeks.

And if you *do* put old boots in, or anything else as tough, be prepared, when you're digging them out, to put them in the bottom of your next heap, because not everything rots down at the same rate. And if you want to spend money on an 'activator', well do so, but a few handfuls of soil scattered on now and

again will do the same thing.

As to how much to use, well I've never seen a garden with too much yet.

When it comes to adding the extra 'magic' to our ground, we must be much more careful. It is near impossible to tell from merely looking at soil what is chemically missing, or what may be there in excess. A study of the plants around, however, can supply some clues if you know what to look for. Rhododendrons and azaleas thriving are a sure sign of an acid tendency. Their absence may mean lime is present. Good, lush, leafy crops point with certainty to enough nitrogen. Good peas and beans and root crops show the phosphate content is right, and well coloured fruit and flowers, enough potash. But the level of these elements is always varying. The crop is always taking them away, and the rains washing them down beyond reach of the roots.

We can assume that they will all be present to some degree in the bare soil itself. Even our simple decomposed compost will partly replace them and, as we have seen, with good fresh farmyard manure to use regularly we need have no fears at all. But without it, we can just as readily assume that we shall have to add them to keep up the fertility level.

It is possible, although it is a longer and more expensive process than might be thought, to have soil analysed. We can be told the exact levels of everything it contains, and how much of everything to add per square yard to put it right. But without such exact knowledge, and without any direct clues that something specific is lacking – for example, scorching round the edges of gooseberry leaves is a sure sign of potash deficiency – it is best to add a fertiliser that contains everything. Compound, or balanced fertilisers as they are known, can be bought as mixtures of inorganic chemicals, or of organic materials 'fortified with' inorganics. And they can be in powder, granular or liquid form, although liquids are generally used for supplementary feeding when the crop is growing.

It is as well, too, to keep small separate quantities. A pound or two of each of the 'big three' will do – nitrogen in the form of sulphate of ammonia, phosphates as superphosphate, and potash as sulphate of potash. These can be used as an extra boost for crops that particularly need them. The cabbage family, for instance, is always partial to a pinch of sulphate of ammonia.

The balance of soil is most likely to be affected by the presence or the absence of lime. Too much of it locks up plant foods and they become unavailable to the plants. Not

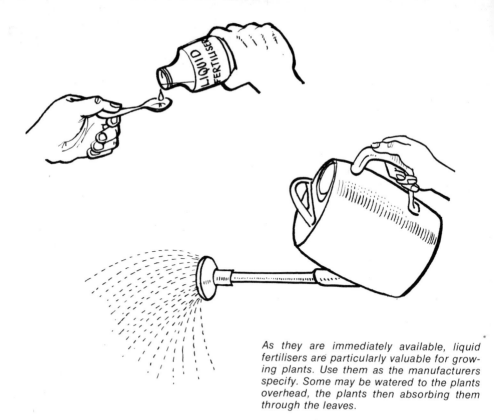

As they are immediately available, liquid fertilisers are particularly valuable for growing plants. Use them as the manufacturers specify. Some may be watered to the plants overhead, the plants then absorbing them through the leaves.

enough of it, and soils become sour with only a very few things living. Of the two the latter is the easiest to correct. Lime can easily be added, but it is difficult to take away, although our yearly additions of humus help in that respect.

It is the easiest of the garden chemicals to monitor in the soil. A simple testing kit can be bought which, if used once a year, will tell immediately if lime is needed. But even this is not essential, and some quite safe assumptions can be made. If lime-hating plants grow well in the district, lime can be applied moderately every year (two or three ounces to the square yard) for most other crops. If rhododendron leaves turn a sickly yellowy green, and hydrangea flowers are a washy pink, lime will only be needed every three or four years perhaps, and then only to counteract the effect of heavy manure dressings.

Finally you may hear something about things referred to almost mysteriously as trace elements. They are materials needed in very minute quantities for plant health. Fortunately, they are another bit of 'magic'

that our star performer farmyard manure supplies. But because this is less used than it was, these traces are sometimes missing.

An absence of boron will produce canker in beetroot, heart rot in celery, and hollow stem in cauliflower. A shortage of copper affects the growing points and the leaves of fruit trees, and causes swollen growth. Where manganese is missing, pale spots develop on potato and beetroot leaves. Magnesium, iron and zinc are other trace elements whose presence is essential. Yet the quantities needed to put things right are very small indeed: 1 ounce to 100 square feet is typical.

The danger is that almost any blot or blemish which is hard to explain away is put down to missing trace elements these days. Don't worry too much, they may never happen. But if you're the worrying sort, spray over and under the leaves of everything with one of the modern liquid foliar fertilisers. They have all the trace elements in them, and if the plants want them, they can absorb them through the leaves.

Chapter 5
Propagation

We have some fun occasionally on *Gardeners' Question Time* when people ask questions about flowers or shrubs which aren't flourishing as they ought to – and then become slightly embarrassed when the team presses for a few more details.

Thus Bill Sowerbutts, Alan Gemmell or Fred Loads may say: 'It's a little difficult to tell why your camellia is failing to flower unless we know a few more details. How old is it? Did you buy it from a garden centre?'

The questioner will blush prettily and stammer something like: 'I'm not sure. I – er – acquired it locally.'

There's a ripple of subdued laughter through the audience. One of their members has been exposed!

Mothers-in-law are particularly skilled in the art of 'crafty cuttings' when they come to tea. You think they've gone to powder their noses when in fact they're in the greenhouse taking the top shoots off your prize pelargoniums.

They've read in their favourite gardening encyclopedia that 'propagation by cuttings is an easy, quick and cheap method of obtaining new plants'.

Come to think of it, my neighbour has a rather attractive variety of begonia which I've been envying for some time. I wonder if I could cut a couple of leaves while his back is turned. First, though, I need to learn something about the art of leaf cutting and, while I'm at it, nodal, root, heel, eye and even Irishman's cutting.

At the same time, let's get to know about the other main methods of propagation – grafting and cultivation from seed.

I suppose there's nothing simpler or cheaper than growing flowers and vegetables from seed. All you do is spend a few pence on a packet of seed, follow the basic instructions on the back (time to sow, depth of drill, distance apart and so on) and hey presto! See how your garden grows.

Nowadays, the slightest risk of failure has been eradicated. For a few pence more you can buy pelleted or taped seeds which ensure there's no need to thin out the seedlings and which 'guarantee' germination.

At least, that's the theory. Strangely enough, it doesn't always work out in practice. Not for me, anyway.

One of the things that's had me flummoxed in the last year or two has been the weather, with mild winters and early warmth in springtime tempting me into sowing too early. In 1974 we had quite hard frosts as late as the end of May.

I try to follow my expert friends' advice, but some of them live in the frozen North and I suppose the time for sowing in, say, Aberdeen must be later than in the kinder climate of rural Berkshire. But how much later? Is there any simple rule to go by?

If seeds need warmth to germinate, they also need moisture – and again the weather has been a positive enemy, with almost freakishly long spells of drought. I watered the flower bed frequently, but I have a nasty feeling that a moist surface and parched subsoil actually do more harm than good to your seedlings.

So what should I do to provide the best conditions for germination? How do I get air into the soil – the other chief ingredient of success with seeds?

Gardening is about living things, which is largely its attraction for me, and in many respects we can produce healthy plants on the same principles as we encourage human vigour – yet my knowledge of germination stemming from the production of six children doesn't seem to be much help!

COLIN HART:
'Multiplication-that's the name of the game'

Once you master the art of raising new plants you well and truly deserve the title of 'green fingers'. There are many ways of propagating. Some are quite conventional, like seeds and stem cuttings. Others, like making cuttings out of roots or even getting leaves to grow, might seem puzzling at first, but really they're quite easy. Let's start with something familiar – seeds.

Blithely following the directions on the glossy seed packets does not mean that everything you sow will immediately spring up like mustard and cress. Far from it! Of course they help, but they are only a brief

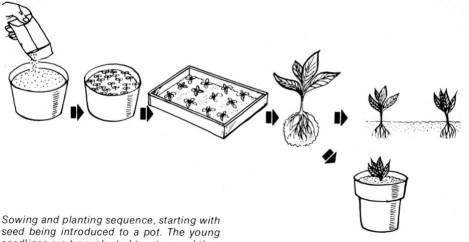

Sowing and planting sequence, starting with seed being introduced to a pot. The young seedlings are transplanted to a tray and then moved with a good amount of earth around the roots into the garden or flowering pot.

guide. Certainly it's best to know what conditions seeds must have for germination before you venture forth with the packet.

Air is one essential requirement. Under glass or indoors the John Innes Seed Compost and the newer composts based on peat won't let you down here because they are nice and open to let air in at the top and water out from the bottom.

Outdoors your troubles (but not necessarily your plants!) can multiply, because you are dealing with ordinary soil. If it's silty a hard crust can seal the surface, and if it's a bit on the sticky side it may easily get waterlogged. If this happens you could find your precious seeds floating away to another part of the garden.

You can safeguard against all this and give your seeds a better start by working peat and sand into the top couple of inches. Peat soaks up the excess water that would otherwise be lying around stagnating, and improves all soils – light or heavy. A coarse, gritty sand does this too but without taking up water, so it's just the job for first-class aeration and drainage.

While we are on the subject of air, always remember to sow seeds thinly. A common cause of seedlings suddenly collapsing is 'damping-off disease'. This often strikes when air cannot freely circulate among the seeds, so be kind and space them out as much as possible.

Very fine greenhouse seeds, like begonias, need to be nursed along gently. Not for them the heavy-handed treatment that their larger companions might put up with. For a start, sowing fine seed really strains your eyes unless you sow directly on a thin layer of silver sand. Then you can see exactly where the seeds have gone and.the sand provides a little extra drainage. Just leave the seeds where they fall – there is no need to press them in or cover with compost.

Now we come to another essential requirement – water. Fine seeds need the upside-down treatment here because overhead watering could wash them away. So when they have been sown, water them from the bottom by plunging the base of the pot or tray in a container of clean water. Leave it there until the surface is wet. It only takes a few minutes for the water to rise up, so don't go away and forget all about it.

Watering gently from above with a fine-rosed can is quite suitable for all the larger seeds, such as lettuce. These should be covered and protected with fine compost, anyway, to a depth roughly equal to their diameter.

Now, to keep the compost moist place a sheet of glass over the container or pop it in a polythene bag. Take it off as soon as you see signs of life, because all seedlings need as much light as possible – except strong sunlight which would be a little unfair at this tender stage.

Outdoors you may have to sow in dry weather, when you may feel obliged to water the seeds afterwards. But this is often wrong!

It is far better to make the drills and pour water along them *before* the seed goes in. The point of all this is that the seeds are nicely bedded down on a moist soil and the roots will delve deep to seek more water. The top layer is dry and loose, but don't worry about this as it stops water from rising to the surface and the young shoots can easily poke their way through to daylight.

And, while we're talking about dry weather, do not forget the birds as they aren't too fussy whether they have wet or dry baths. Black cotton criss-crossed just above the seed will keep them away.

Large seeds like sweet pea, marrow and cucumber are designed for fumbling fingers, as they are big enough to sow individually. Spacing them out gives each one its own little growing area and, if they go direct into small pots, the tedious task of pricking out the seedlings is done away with altogether.

Nowadays many of the smaller flower and vegetable seeds don't have to be pricked out if you buy them in those transparent blister packs. True the seeds look large, but only because each one has been pelleted with an inert material so you can sow them one by one. Pelleted seed must be kept slightly moister than ordinary seed so that water can pass right through them.

Taped seeds simplify matters even more, as you just lay the tape in position and water it. This rots down, leaving the seeds to grow at the correct spacings. It really makes sowing child's play, but you still need to get the soil in the right condition first.

As for the difference in sowing times in various parts of the country, gardeners in the south have the edge over their northern counterparts who might be two or three weeks behind. But, wherever you live, always be guided by the weather, as seedlings which have had to struggle in the cold are often overtaken by those sown later in better conditions.

If you don't get on well with seeds – and not everyone does – why not try cuttings? You will have no bother at all with easy subjects like dahlias and chrysanthemums. Some houseplants, like ivies, Busy Lizzie and Wandering Jew, will root in water!

Softwood or leafy stem cuttings are taken during late spring and summer from plants like catmint and pansies, which never become woody. Only select the healthiest and sturdiest growths which are not going to flower and cut them about 3 inches long.

Nodal cuttings root best, so trim them with a sharp knife just below a node (the junction

Nodal cuttings are taken just below a node – the point where a leaf joins the stem.

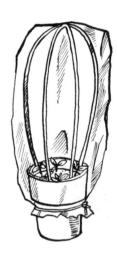

A miniature propagation case can easily be made by securing a polythene bag over the pot, supported by a wire frame.

where a leaf joins the stem). This is where most of the roots will come.

Always remove the bottom leaves to stop them from rotting.

A hormone rooting powder can work

wonders with cuttings if you haven't quite got that 'green-fingered' touch. Some even contain a fungicide to help keep stem rots at bay.

If you don't feel like lashing out on a compost in which to root your cuttings, you can make your own at home. Just combine peat and sharp sand together in equal quantities and you will have a mixture that will suit nearly everything, because it's nice and open, but still holds water: and you don't need any fertiliser.

All you have to do now is put the cuttings in a pot, pan or tray so that they are not quite touching each other, and then carefully water once to firm them in.

The next thing is to keep the foliage damp, otherwise the leaves will quickly wilt and dry out. So pop the whole container in a clear polythene bag and tie the top. If you like you can use a propagating frame. Really this is just a box covered with glass or polythene to keep the air humid.

Cuttings must have good light while they are rooting but direct sunlight would be most unkind, so pick a semi-shaded spot in the greenhouse.

Heat helps them to root, and for most subjects 60 - 65°F is comfortable. Below this they may take longer, but they shouldn't come to any harm unless they get too cold. And then they might rot.

You should be able to tell when cuttings have rooted – without pulling them up – by looking at their tops. When you see new growth there, gradually give the cuttings some air so that after a few days the polythene or glass covering can come off altogether.

Some cuttings are called semi-ripe because they are taken towards the end of the summer when they are neither soft nor hard. Examples include berberis, viburnum, fuchsia, hydrangea and geranium. It is possible to pull some shrubby cuttings off so that they come away with a wedge-shaped piece of the older wood attached. You then have a 'heel cutting' and there is no need to trim these to just below a node. Sometimes they strike better this way. Make all the semi-ripe cuttings about 3 inches long and root them the same way as for softwood cuttings. Geraniums often do better just stuck under the staging without any covering, as too much moisture makes them rot. Watch the drips though!

Hardwood, or ripe cuttings are the odd ones out. They have to be long – about 10 inches in fact – as they are slower to root and need a reserve of food to tide them over the winter. They are taken in the autumn after leaf-fall,

when their shoots are hard and woody, from trees and shrubs like willow, poplar and roses. Trim below a node, as usual, but since there are no leaves to worry about root them in a sandy, protected spot outdoors.

Put them in firmly with only one-third of the cutting above ground. New shoots will spring up later from the buried buds to give bushy plants. The exceptions are red and white currants and gooseberries, which are grown on 'legs'. To get these, strip off all but the top three buds and then plant the cuttings. This prevents the dense suckering growth that would otherwise smother the bushes and make picking difficult. Rooting hardwood cuttings is a slow job, so be prepared to leave them alone for a year.

While we're on the subject of stem cuttings, don't forget that there are other types. Begonia rex and gloxinias can be grown from leaves. Just take a healthy, almost mature leaf and lay it face down on a sheet of glass. With a razor blade slit the main veins every couple of inches apart. Now turn the leaf face up in a tray filled with moist, sandy compost. Stop it from curling by pegging it down with hairpins, or by putting a couple of small stones on top, and then cover it with the glass. Given warmish conditions a new plant should spring up from each slit.

Leaf petiole cuttings are less tricky. Take whole leaves, with about 1½ inches of stalk attached, from African violets and peperomias. Insert them upright so that the base of each leaf is just above the compost. With warmth and humidity little plantlets form at the base of the leaves.

Cuttings can also be taken from the part of the plants that you see the least of anyway – the roots! Phlox, Anchusa italica, gypsophila, oriental poppy, horseradish and seakale can be propagated this way – in fact, almost anything with fairly fleshy roots. Chop them up into 3-inch lengths in the autumn and place them upright about 2 inches down in a sandy compost in a cold frame or cool greenhouse. When you're cutting them up make a straight cut across the top and a sloping one at the bottom. This way you shouldn't go wrong by planting them upside-down. Later on, in the spring, the new plants can be potted up ready for planting out the following autumn.

Finally what must be the simplest way to propagate – Irishman's Cuttings. Really they are just rooted suckers which you pull off border plants like chrysanthemums and michaelmas daisies in the spring. And with the luck of the Irish some of them might even flower that autumn.

Chapter 6
Vegetables

A remarkable number of horticultural societies around the country have lately been celebrating either the 60th or the 35th anniversary of their birth.

In other words, they came into existence at the beginning of the First or Second World Wars. 'Dig for Victory' was the slogan which spurred neighbourly groups to get together and produce as many fresh vegetables as they could.

Being a great age, I can well remember the posters during the war against Germany and Japan, exhorting us to grow potatoes and carrots and all the other vegetables which would provide the much-needed vitamins that basic food rationing didn't.

Growing our own food was also supposed to take the strain off our heroic merchant seamen by cutting down food imports.

After that war, there was a natural swing back to flowers and away from vegetables. Now the pendulum has swung yet again because we have a new economic war on our hands.

Apart from those years when patriotism was the spur, I've never been much of a vegetable grower. Buying from the greengrocer seemed cheaper than producing my own – and the quality was usually better.

(My wife is particularly sensitive to creepy-crawlies and my cauliflowers and cabbages were usually full of the things.)

Now, however, shop prices have soared to such dizzy heights that our garden is once again full of lettuces and leeks, carrots and courgettes, tomatoes and turnips. I expect yours is, too.

Yet I haven't really the foggiest idea whether I'm growing the right varieties, and studying the latest catalogues serves only to deepen the confusion, especially as there are so many new names to conjure with.

I like the idea of the Burpless Cucumber with its soft and tender skin which doesn't need peeling (or repeating, presumably), but would I be more sensible cultivating one of the disease-resistant varieties of 'very strong constitution'?

How am I to choose between no fewer than 20 varieties of lettuce in just one catalogue whose qualities are said to include 'extraordinary' size, heavy hearts, hardiness, tenderness, crispness and compactness, not to mention fimbriated leaves, whatever they may be?

The whole business of growing vegetables has become so much more sophisticated. An important factor now, for instance, is the suitability of different crops for deep freezing, though I confess to a certain cynicism about the much-vaunted 'freshness' of frozen foods.

But I mustn't pretend to be too ignorant. I'm actually proud of my successes with tomatoes grown by the hydroponic method in the greenhouse. May I tell you about it?

I fill 6-inch clay pots with 'sharp' sand, obtained from my friendly neighbourhood builder, to within half an inch of the lip. In this wholly inorganic holding agent, I place the small tomato plants and arrange the pots in rows along the plastic-covered bench which runs the whole length of the greenhouse.

Then I simply feed the plants every day with a nutrient solution, known in the Barratt household as 'Dad's Goo'. It contains things like nitrogen, phosphoric acid, potash, magnesium, manganese and iron.

Getting the proportions right is, of course, a problem far beyond my scientific capabilities, so for my first season I had it made by a friend of mine who grew acres of tomatoes and carnations by this method under glass.

When he moved from the district, I thought my hydroponic days were over, but I came upon other feeds from retailers, which proved to be just as effective.

End of story – except for the usual basic jobs of removing side shoots, supporting the plants (in my case, with strings suspended from the greenhouse roof), and encouraging the fruits to set by lightly brushing the flowers with an artist's paint brush.

I've also been having a go with the new compost bags as a variation on soilless cultivation.

When one company introduced bags, it said:

'The product should enable the newcomer growing for the first time to obtain successful crops, and you can expect the newcomer to abuse the product, so it was very necessary to achieve a high degree of tolerance to mis-use.'

Now that's what I'm really after – vegetable-growing methods which will be guaranteed to succeed despite the abuse of novices like me . . .

BILL TAYLOR:
'Grow vegetables that suit your soil'

I am pretty certain that a gardening book with the words 'Down-to-Earth' in its title must be referring in the main to its vegetable section! Surely it's here where you have more than a nodding acquaintance with the good soil itself. You dig it over; you feed it; you get it under your finger nails and on your clothes. After all that you finish up by loving it. And why? Because you get to understand both its potential and its limitations.

Try to grow vegetables that suit your soil. All the root crops, such as parsnips, carrots, beetroots, potatoes, etc, thrive on sandy soil. Onions also do well, providing you can keep them watered.

Brassicas (by which I mean all the cabbage family, especially brussel sprouts and cauliflowers) are not happy on sand. They like to take a firm grip with their roots and, as they all have large leaves which can lever the plant up in a strong wind, you can't altogether blame them!

Peas and beans (called legumes) prefer a stiffer soil such as a well-worked clay but, as with the roots and the brassicas, it doesn't mean that they will not grow on other types of soil, but simply that they don't prefer them.

Digging is probably the most important, and certainly the hardest, job in the vegetable garden. I have known a good many gardeners who say they enjoy it, but I may add they were all professionals and went about the job in a different manner to the average allottee.

First of all, they always kept their spades sharp and clean. Not for them the scraping of the blade after every two or three spits. Their blades almost slipped into the ground, with hardly any pressure from the foot, and when the spit of soil was turned it was rolled over, and not lifted more than 2 or 3 inches.

The secret of easy digging is to start off correctly. Firstly, always take out a digging trench approximately 18 inches wide by 10 to 12 inches deep. Barrow the soil to where you plan to stop digging so that it can be used to fill the last row you dig. If the land to be dug over is just a narrow strip in between other crops you can carry the soil on the spade. The important point is not only to make the work easy, but also to keep the land level.

Much has been talked and written about the benefits of double digging, but after a lifetime of gardening both as a professional and as an amateur, I have come to the conclusion that the bottom spit is best left where it is. The top spit is the most important. This is where manures and fertilisers should go, not downstairs where the soil is almost sterile.

Don't get me wrong. I am not against breaking up the lower spit and I do so for two reasons – firstly to crack the hard pan and enable excess water to drain away, and secondly so that during a period of drought moisture can, by capillary action, be brought to the surface area. My method of breaking the bottom spit is to drive the spade in at 6-inch intervals along the bottom of the digging trench and simply move it backwards and forwards until the soil is loose. No turning of the spit is done.

I cannot overstress the importance of doing as much digging as possible before the winter sets in. Frost is a wonderful soil conditioner and the natural settling of the soil is very important.

Adding compost or manure when digging doesn't necessarily mean putting it at the bottom of the digging trench. It is far better to slope towards you the spit of soil you have just turned over and put the compost on this slope so that it reaches from the bottom to the top. This encourages plants to send their roots outwards not downwards. In other words, instead of the compost being horizontal at the bottom of the trench it is nearly vertical and plants can take advantage of it while they are still fairly young.

Let's have a look at Michael's remark about there being too many varieties of vegetables to grow.

It is a valid point, but what suits one person doesn't necessarily suit another, nor the situation of the garden for that matter. His choice of lettuce as an example is very apt. I am pretty certain that we all have our likes and dislikes about lettuce. For instance, I like the small, hard Little Jem, whereas my wife's choice is the large Cos type. Yet another member of our family prefers the large crinkly Great Lakes or Webbs Wonderful. So my answer is to grow a

A splendid crop of cabbages with uniform solid hearts makes the hard work of ground preparation more than worthwhile.

few of each!

The fimbriated-leaved lettuce Michael mentions is an American loose-leaf variety called Salad Bowl and, if you like it, it can be a useful vegetable to grow. You can actually remove one leaf at a time from a plant and, as this variety does not readily go to seed, it is handy if you have a small garden and are fond of salads.

It is as well that there are many different kinds of vegetables. Some are early maturing, others late, and seedsmen do state this in their catalogues. It's up to you to make your choice.

Creepy crawlies! What a graphic description of the bugs and caterpillars in Michael's garden. I know exactly what he means, and who doesn't? But surely it's his own fault. Almost all seed shops these days could be mistaken for chemists from the number of bottles one sees on the shelves. There is an insecticide for every pest, but it is no good just giving one application and thinking that has put paid to them for good. Far from it. You may have killed the 'creepy crawlies' that were there but not their eggs, which in a few days hatch out and you are back to square one. Make no mistake about it; if you want clean vegetables then you must be prepared to undertake a regular spraying programme.

What about the mysteries of rotational cropping of vegetables? Most beginners and quite a lot of experienced gardeners simply flout nature by being haphazard and growing the same kind of vegetable year after year on the same patch of ground.

This, as can be imagined, upsets the balance of soil fertility and after a while good crops of that particular vegetable cannot be grown. If other crops are produced on that patch in rotation then the soil has time to recover. In practice it has been proved that a three-year rotation is ample, and it seems a simple matter to divide the garden into three equal sections. But it isn't as straightforward as it sounds, for a family may not be fond of a lot of potatoes and roots. And if you have a third of the garden delegated for these, then you either let part of that section go to waste or are tempted to grow something extra from the other sections, especially if you are fond of peas or beans for instance.

In this case, my advice is by all means to move the brassicas and potato families on to fresh ground every third year, but do not worry too much about the peas, onions or beans and the various other things that go to make a vegetable garden. A two-year rotation for these, providing you maintain soil fertility,

will get you by.

Now let's take a look at the actual cultivation of vegetables, starting with potatoes. If ever a vegetable required plenty of compost and fertilisers, this is it. The weight of crop compared with any other vegetable is fantastic, and very much depends on the amount of compost used.

The soil should be dug over in the winter and left rough. In the spring, trenches are taken out 18 inches wide and 9 inches deep. Deposit a good 6-inch layer of compost with a good handful of potato fertiliser scattered every 3 feet or so. Now place your seed potatoes on the compost 18 or 15 inches apart, according to whether they are late or early

Drills for seeds can be made with the edge of a hoe (top), a rake (centre) or by scraping away the top surface with a spade.

varieties. The distance between trenches will again vary – 30 inches for the lates, 24 inches for the earlies.

It always pays to lay out your potatoes in boxes in March in a frostproof room with plenty of light. This allows the eyes to sprout and when you plant in mid-April these shoots should be about an inch long. To prevent damage to the shoots, carefully cover them over with a handful of soil before shovelling in the remaining earth. The plants will want ridging up with a hoe when about 12 inches high.

Carrots and beetroots should always be included in this section of the garden as they do better if rotated properly.

The favourite here is the carrot, and as they have to swell within the ground it stands to reason that the soil should not be too firm. When raking over the land to level it prior to sowing in April, scatter four ounces to the square yard of superphosphate of lime and rake it into the surface. Roots require phosphates and these come into operation almost immediately.

Sow thinly and not too deeply, and always dust with a repellent in order to keep away carrot fly, especially when thinning. The rows should be 9 inches apart.

Beetroot is said to be a maritime plant, a native of the sea shore. Just notice how the ornamental beetroots thrive in the flower beds at any seaside resort. They simply stand out. To help them feel at home in your garden just add a little ordinary table salt to the superphosphate of lime. A level teaspoonful to the square yard is ample.

Never sow beetroot before mid-April. If you do the chances are that it will go to seed before it is fit enough to pull.

The brassica family comes next in importance, as with reasonable luck you can cut greens of some description every day of the year.

This is the section of land that needs an annual dressing of lime, as the grandfather of all the brassicas – the wild cabbage – still lives in the chalky soil of the south of England.

Brassicas thrive best on soil that has been manured the previous season. Fresh manure sends them rank. Brussel sprouts, cabbages, cauliflowers, broccoli, etc, can be sown in the open in early April and planted out in their permanent places in mid-June. With a greenhouse you can get an earlier crop by sowing at the beginning of March and planting out early in May. Don't forget to treat the planting holes with Gamma Dust, which will keep the plants free from the maggots of the cabbage root fly.

Long and short-horn carrots – a real delicacy fresh from the garden.

Here again planting distances are important and there is nothing gained by putting the rows too close. All brassicas need space to develop their outside leaves if you want them to heart up properly in the case of cabbages, or make nice curds in cauliflowers. As far as sprouts go, without large leaves you will not get firm buttons.

Firm ground is required, too, especially for sprouts where there should be no less than 2½ to 3 feet between plants and between rows. This gives you an opportunity to grow lettuce, spinach, radish, etc, in between as these will be up before the sprouts take over. Cabbages, cauliflowers and the like require at least 1½ feet between them.

Onions, leeks and shallots are all well worth growing, especially if you like soups and stews, although shallots are mostly pickled. Again, rich ground is required and, if a few forks full of manure can be added when digging, so much the better. The exceptions are shallots, which for some reason do not keep if treated too well.

The site for onions must be open and sunny, well away from overhanging trees and shrubs. This vegetable requires plenty of phosphates and potash, and a good foundation is provided by a dressing of equal parts of superphosphate of lime and sulphate of potash. Four to six ounces of the mixture to the square yard should be scattered over the surface in February or March, sooner if the surface is dry, and well raked in.

You can sow onion seeds in a greenhouse early in the year or outside in April, depending on how important the crop is to you. Onion sets can be purchased from almost any seed shop. Plant the sets 9 inches apart, pushed halfway into the ground, in the same way that

1st year	2nd year	3rd year
onions	Peas/Early	celery
Shallots	cabbage	Potatoes
Peas M/crop	Savoy	Beet
Beans	Brussels	carrots
celery	Broccoli	Parsnips
Potatoes	onions	Peas/Early
Beet	Shallots	cabbage
carrots	Peas M/crop	Savoy
Parsnip	Beans	Brussels
Peas/Early	celery	Broccoli
cabbage	Potatoes	onions
Savoy	Beet	Shallots
Brussels	carrots	Peas M/crop
Broccoli	Parsnips	Beans

A typical three-year crop rotation plan.

42

you do shallots. Keep weeds away and you can harvest bulbs weighing over 8 ounces each in September.

Leeks follow the same pattern but, when planting out in May, make a hole with a dibber about 6 inches deep, pop the plant in and fill the hole with water to settle the roots at the bottom.

Peas and beans, like the brassicas, need lime in the soil as well as phosphates and if a little compost can be spared and trenched in you are more than halfway to a successful crop. Sow the early varieties at the beginning of March in 6-inch wide drills, 1 inch deep, scattering the peas in but keeping each seed at least 2 inches from its neighbour. Before covering over, scatter 1 ounce of Basic Slag along each yard of drill, and it doesn't matter if it goes on the seeds. This will supply both lime and phosphates in a suitable form. After

covering in, walk on the soil to make firm.

Distance between rows is fairly simple to work out as all varieties have the height to which they will grow marked on the packet. If more than one row is required of the same variety, the stated height is the distance between rows. Twiggy sticks from the hedgerows are ideal to hold peas upright.

Early peas, usually round seeded, can go in the ground in January to February, second earlies in March and April, main crop in May.

Beans, both runner and dwarf, are very vulnerable to frost and must not be planted in the open until all danger of frost is past. Seeds, however, go in after the first week in May and by the time they come through the ground all danger of frost is over.

To assist drainage, and also to allow moisture to rise by capillary action in dry conditions, the bottom spit can be broken up by inserting a spade and working it backwards and forwards.

For easy digging take out a trench 18 inches wide by 10-12 inches deep and barrow the soil to the other end of the digging area, so that it can be used to fill the last row.

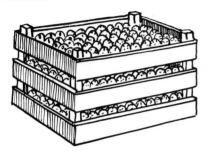

It always pays to lay out potatoes in boxes in March in a light, frost-proof room to allow the eyes to sprout.

Runner beans require a trench taken out roughly 2 feet deep and the bottom filled with anything that retains moisture, such as pieces of old carpet, hessian bags or newspaper. After a good dusting over with lime to keep it sweet, the subsoil is replaced first, followed by the richer top soil, to which is added a fair amount of manure or compost with an occasional dusting of bone meal.

Broad and dwarf beans need exactly the same treatment as peas, both in ground preparation and the distance between rows. The only difference is that the seeds are put further apart, round about 9 inches from seed to seed and slightly deeper. In the case of

You can give broad beans an early start by sowing in individual peat pots in a greenhouse in winter. However, the seed is virtually frost-proof and may also be sown outdoors at this time.

broad beans, these are virtually frost proof and can be sown in the depth of winter, always providing the ground isn't actually frozen over! In the south of England it's always a good bet to make a sowing in late September or October and, providing Jack Frost is in a good mood, it is possible to have beans on your plate in the following May.

Chapter 7
Fruit

When we lived in Nigeria, the compound of our mud house was a riot of colour. Fruit blossom in particular was a joy to behold.

And then, in the space of a few hours, flowers and leaves alike had disappeared. We'd been visited by a swarm of locusts which ate their fill and then moved on, leaving us with nothing but bare branches.

It was one of the many times that I longed for dear old Britain, for blossom in the springtime, for the Vale of Evesham at its loveliest, for greenery untouched by the ravages of tropical pests.

Now, home again, I wander round the garden savouring the delights of the orchard and the soft fruit. There are weevils in my apples, capsid on the cherries, sawfly and codling moth burrowing into the plums, beetles in the raspberries, and slugs and snails making a meal of my strawberries.

I'm keeping a wary eye open for mildew and midge, woolly aphids, red spider, greenfly, blackfly, big bud, grey mould, brown rot, canker, scab, moth caterpillars, peach leaf curl . . . No, I won't go on. It's altogether too painful.

Let's talk about sex instead.

When I was at school, I learned that pollen was the powder discharged from the anther of a male flower and that, if a bee, or a breeze, transferred it to the pistil of another flower, fertilisation would be effected.

But I didn't get much further than that. How do you tell, for instance, whether a flower is male or female? Can you get both on the same fruit tree? What's to be done to encourage fertility if there's a shortage of bees and breezes?

Is it necessary to have two trees or bushes of the same fruit to ensure cross-fertilisation? How is it that some fruits appear to be self-fertilising?

I've been trying to follow one of those 'year-at-a-glance' type guides to looking after my fruit and there are many more questions to which I'd like answers.

It says, for instance, that March is the month for planting raspberries and strawberries. Yes, but how? And where?

In April I'm advised to 'keep a watch for pests on flowers and fruitlets'. But what precisely am I looking for, and what preventive action can I take before it's too late?

May's the time to bark ring apples and pears if necessary to encourage fruiting. I do wish somebody would tell me how – and why this method should give me a bigger or better crop.

Even when the advice is as simple as June's – 'harvest strawberries' – I'm still perplexed. Assuming you have a heavy crop, what's the best method of storing them? What's the best way to prepare them for deep freezing?

I'd better stop before the question mark falls off my hard-pressed typewriter . . .

LES JONES:
'Observation and anticipation are the keys'

Growing fruit of any kind can give a lifetime of pleasure, for the cropping life of a fruit tree, bush, cane or plant extends from three years in the case of the strawberry to 40 years for the well-managed apple tree. Thoughtful planning is of primary importance, for the major difference between growing fruit and growing vegetable crops is that mistakes are more difficult and costly to rectify, and it may be three or five years before you even realise that the mistake has been made.

Correct spacing is essential if the tree or bush is to flourish, and the decision on how many types of fruit can be grown, and where, will be dictated by the size of your garden and the proportion allocated to fruit cultivation. When planning your garden bear in mind that many fruits can play a dual role, particularly if space is limited. Fan-trained forms of pears, plums, peaches, nectarines, cherries, red and white currants and gooseberries can be planted for a decorative effect, but fan-trained trees do need to be at least 12 feet apart, so it is not always possible to fit them into your layout. However, apples, pears, gooseberries and red and white currants can be purchased as single or double cordons which only require 2½ to 3 feet between them, so you should be able to fit a couple of these into your scheme, even if the available area is restricted.

Fences, particularly those with three or four strands of galvanised wire, reinforced with a few 2-inch by 1-inch battens as spacers, will make ideal bases for training loganberries, blackberries and cordons.

Siting is important, as soil, light, and protection from wind and frost all play a part in the successful production of fruit. In a large garden you can take advantage of the best positions – a south- or west-facing aspect, away from the lowest ground (which might be subject to late frosts and waterlogging during winter).

In a small garden no such choice exists, so a careful study must be made of which areas are shaded, exposed to full sun, wet, dry, or in the path of wind, which is often funnelled between houses. You can then select suitable fruits for the different situations.

All fruit needs well-drained, well-manured soil. Clay soil creates most problems, but if the drainage is right most fruits will do well and produce good crops. Blackcurrants will tolerate the wetter conditions, but raspberries and strawberries would not enjoy them, so some grit, coarse sand, leaf soil, peat, garden compost or farmyard manure must be worked into the soil to improve drainage before planting.

Lighter soils, such as sands and gravels, are easily worked and seldom present drainage problems; but they do have a tendency to dry out just when moisture is most needed. Lack of humus is the problem here, and priority must therefore be given to building this up again; heavy dressings of bulk organics need to be applied before planting and used continually afterwards as mulches.

Chalk and limestone soils will need similar treatment, for they are usually thin and poor, and your fruit would almost certainly suffer from iron and manganese deficiency.

Good loams are, of course, ideal for fruit growing, as they usually contain a reasonable percentage of organic matter and food reserve. But it is as well to remember that even the best soil suffers from lack of essential ingredients at some time, so this aspect should never be neglected.

Lime content is also important: too much will lead to deficiency problems, but a small annual or biennial application will do no harm.

The final preparation for planting can be made in September and October when most soils work well. Apply either 3 ounces of superphosphate or 1 ounce of sulphate of potash per square yard; the superphosphate can be replaced by bone meal, or by a mixture of 2 ounces of hoof and horn, 3 ounces of bone meal and 1 ounce of sulphate of potash per square yard. Whichever is used it should be worked well into the soil by forking or rotovating.

The term 'top fruit' is a collective one used for apples, pears, plums, gages, damsons, peaches, nectarines and cherries. All these will form large trees if allowed to grow naturally, but to bring some order into the size, shape and cropping potential of these fruits, a great deal of research work has been, and still is, being carried out. Although the results are produced primarily for the commercial fruit growing industry, the amateur can also reap the benefits of this work.

The trees are propagated by budding the cultivar (a man-made variety produced by hybridisation) on to one of the classified rootstocks, so that any fruit tree you purchase has, in fact, been attached to special root systems. The potential of each root system is well known so that all trees on a particular rootstock will be identical in size and cropping ability. Therefore, when selecting fruit for your garden, you should ask on what rootstock the trees have been worked, as this will give you a fairly accurate guide to ultimate size, etc.

With apples the rootstock are divided into four groups – Very Dwarfing, Dwarfing, Vigorous and Very Vigorous. For a small garden, choose Very Dwarfing stocks, but if you want a specimen tree to provide shade, or a future support for the hammock or children's swings, then select a Very Vigorous stock. For general use Very Dwarfing stock, Malling 9 and Malling 26 are most useful. Dwarfing stocks Malling 7 and Malling Merton 106 provide a medium vigorous tree, while for strong growing larger trees you will need Malling 2 and Malling Merton 11.

Cordons have a single stem, with the fruit spurs developed along its length. Apples and pears are trained as cordons.

An espalier will have a central stem with pairs of opposite branches growing out at right angles to the main stem; again, apples and pears can be obtained as espaliers.

Fan-trained trees live up to their name. A short stem of 12 to 18 inches is trained so that a number of branches radiate outwards to form a fan. Apples and pears are seldom trained in this form, but it is widely used for apricots, plums, gages, peaches, nectarines and cherries.

The bush is the most common shape in fruit trees, with a stem of three feet or so topped by a framework of branches, well spaced to form a balanced head.

To form a half standard a stem of 4½ to 5 feet is built up, and then the branch work is as for the bush tree. A full standard is similar but will have a 6- to 7-foot stem.

Cordons are planted 2½ to 3 feet apart in a row, with 7 to 8 feet between rows.

Bush trees on Malling 9 or 26 are planted 8 to 10 feet apart, but if worked on Malling 2 the distance should be 15 to 20 feet.

Fan-trained trees need to be 12 to 15 feet apart, and espaliers on Dwarfing stock Malling 106 the same. But if they are worked on Malling 2 or Malling 111 20 feet would not be excessive.

When the trees arrive plant them immediately – this is not a long job if the ground has been prepared and stakes and tying material are at hand. Start by digging a hole large enough to allow the roots to spread evenly, and deep enough to sit the tree at the original depth (indicated by the soil mark on the stem).

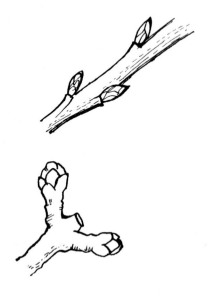

Different buds on fruit trees: growth buds (top) and fruit buds (bottom).

If you are planting a bush or a half standard that needs a stake, put the stake in the centre of the hole and drive it in until it is quite firm. Then place the tree against it in a planting position, check the height of the lowest branches, and put a mark on the stake 3 inches below the branch. Remove the tree and saw off the top of the stake. Now plant the tree, working the soil in gradually and firming the earth as you go. Finally, attach the tie loosely so that any settling can take place without the tree being restricted.

All fruit trees have male and female parts present in each individual flower. When pollen is transferred from the stamens of one flower to the stigma of another, cross pollination is said to occur, while transference of pollen from the stamens to the stigma of the same flower is called self-pollination. If a tree is described as self-fertile, its pollen, when placed on the stigma of the tree, will produce fertilisation. If a tree is described as self-sterile, then pollen must be brought from other trees, either by insects or artificially, before fertilisation can take place.

I shall not go into the details of each cultivar here but, for example, when more than one apple tree is planted, as long as the flowering periods coincide at some point there should be no pollination problem. With pears, plums, gages and cherries pollinators are more important, and you can usually find detailed information on these species in fruit nurserymen's catalogues.

Lack of pollination is often blamed for small or even non-existent crops but, in my experience, this is seldom the cause of crop failure, particularly in urban areas. So, before blaming the lack of suitable pollinators, take a close look at these possible alternatives.

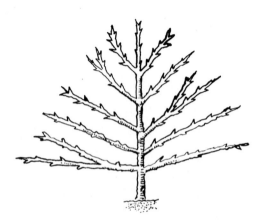

Where blossom is good but no fruit set follows, frost may well be the culprit, as small gardens are often frost pockets.

Another reason for poor crops may be an early attack of aphids and suckers feeding within the green cluster. This will often do sufficient damage to cause collapse of flower stalks at, or immediately after, petal fall.

In residential areas the tree may be so situated that it is subject to wind funnelled between houses, which prevents pollinating insects from doing their job.

Late spraying, or spraying with incorrect material, will damage flower trusses and pollinating insects, and even the use of strong smelling sprays in close proximity to the tree will deter insects.

Very dry atmospheric conditions destroy the pollen on wall-trained trees during periods of hot sunshine, so a light spray over with clean water is advised during the flowering period.

In the first year after planting, cut out any surplus and weak branchlets, but always aim to leave well-spaced, vigorous young shoots. Having selected those you want to keep, cut them back to a good firm bud (preferably outward facing), halfway down the shoot.

On bushes, fans and espaliers, the same pruning will have to be repeated the following winter, and all the side shoots should be cut back to two or three buds.

In the third year on bush trees, cordons, espaliers and fan-trained trees of all types in a small garden, change to summer pruning. This gives you more control over the formation of the tree and its vigour, and it also encourages the development of fruit buds. Apples, pears, plums, apricots and cherries will respond to summer pruning, which is car-

ried out from mid-July through to August. If the young shoots are not wanted for extension growths to increase the size of the tree, they are cut back to five or six leaves. This checks the growth of the tree and many of the buds on the remaining part of the shoot will form fruit buds.

The exceptions to this form of pruning are peaches and nectarines, for these produce fruit not on spurs, but on the young wood, so a different technique must be used. When the young wood of the previous year breaks into growth in the spring and the shoots are about 1 to 1½ inches long, a process called disbudding is carried out.

Look at each fruiting branch (those which bear flowers) and select two good shoots at the base, one in the centre portion of the branch, and the leading shoot. Remove all the remaining young shoots, although you can retain a few more if you like as long as you stop them at two leaves.

Standard apple and pear trees are pruned in November to December. Remove crossing branches and weak wood, together with any surplus branches likely to cause overcrowding.

Plums, gages and cherries are pruned in full leaf during late May and early June; this early pruning reduces the risk of disease.

Some winter pruning will also be required on apples and pears which have been summer pruned, but it is minimal and consists of cutting back any secondary growth or overlooked shoots, plus any fruit spurs or overcrowding shoots.

Soft fruits is the collective term used for currants, gooseberries, raspberries, loganberries, blackberries and strawberries.

Blackcurrants should always be grown as a

Classified rootstocks produce trees of specific size and shape. From left to right: fan-trained; standard; cordon; espalier; bush.

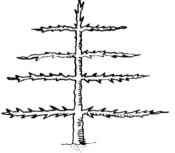

stool, ie, with a large number of branches arising from below soil level.

Red and white currants and gooseberries need to be grown on a clean stem, 12 to 18 inches in length with a semi-permanent branch work. The bushes should be planted at least 4 feet apart, with 6 feet between rows (single cordons 2 feet apart, double cordons 3 feet), either against a wall between developing fan-trained trees, or in a row across the plot, supported by two wires secured to strong posts at each end, and a single 7-foot cane to each cordon.

Raspberries should be planted with 18 inches between stools and 6 inches between rows. The support is three wires at 18 inches above soil level, one at 5 feet, and another in between. Lack of space may prevent you planting a full row, but an alternative is to plant four canes around a central stake, preferably iron, and to support them with loops of string taken round the canes and attached to the stake.

The advantage of this system is that is allows a more manageable quantity to be grown, simplifies the control of perennial weeds and disease, and is more convenient for picking, pruning and tying in.

Loganberries and blackberries must be trained on a fence-like structure made from five or six strands of wire, or against a wall as fans. Both these fruits are extremely vigorous and will cover 12 to 15 feet of fence or wall per plant. Raspberries, loganberries and blackberries crop on the young canes produced the previous year.

Blackcurrants, raspberries, loganberries and blackberries crop on the previous year's wood, and all are pruned immediately after the fruit has been gathered.

By pruning annually in this way and at this time, a continual supply of young wood is produced, which ripens before the onset of winter. If growth is poor an application of sulphate of ammonia (2 ounces per square yard), followed by a through watering will encourage stronger wood.

If gooseberries and white and red currants are grown as bushes, pruning is carried out in the late winter, usually February, when you should remove the young wood and cut the lateral shoots (side shoots on the main branches) to two buds. The leaders are reduced by a third if the bushes are still developing, otherwise cut back as with the laterals.

This group of soft fruits suffers from potash deficiency in almost every garden; the tell-tale symptom of this is scorched edges

A nice stem of blackcurrant ready for picking. After the harvest the old wood is taken out as next year's fruit will be borne on the new shoots.

around the leaves in June and July. Apply 1 ounce of sulphate of potash per square yard in February to correct this disorder.

The last of the popular fruits is the strawberry, which has the shortest life, as the beds need renewing every three years.

Planting of strawberries ought to be completed in August if the young plants are to be cropped the following year. If the plants are

Still one of the most popular apples in Britain, Cox's Orange Pippin has a beautiful colour and a sweet flavour.

healthy and have cropped well, then planting runners (young plantlets) can be lifted direct from the old bed or some of the earliest runners can be established in 3-inch pots and allowed to root. After rooting sever them from the mother plant.

However, if there is any sign of stunted plants, small fruits which fail to ripen, or of curled, mottled or yellow leaves, a new stock should be purchased from a reputable grower supplying certified plants. These plants will not arrive until October no matter how early your order is placed, so no crop can be taken the first year.

As this plant is moved at least every third year, it should be included in the rotation of the vegetable garden, and the site from which the early potatoes have been lifted makes an ideal spot for the new planting.

Level and firm the soil, apply a dressing of complete fertiliser, and (for the three-year system) plant runners 18 inches apart with 30 inches between the rows.

The one-year system has much to commend it but early planting is essential, preferably by August 10. Plant in double rows 12 inches apart and at 15-inch intervals between the rows; if more than one double row is planted allow 24 inches between rows. Once the crop has been picked, runners are selected for planting and pegged down with pieces of U-shaped wire. When the runners have rooted they are planted, while the old plants are cleared and burned.

The advantages of the one-year system are that it allows for cloching if a few early berries are required, and it avoids the weedy, overgrown strawberry bed with all the tedious cleaning work which the three-year bed entails.

Pests and diseases are always to the fore by about mid-June. Complete control is never achieved and should not, in my view, be attempted. But some control is advisable and necessary if you are to get clean fruit. With top fruit, sprays are applied in winter, spring and summer. Tar oil is the standard winter wash and controls a wide range of insect eggs, while keeping the trees clean. Use it every second or third year on all fruit except strawberries, but use it early – from late November to the end of December. If you leave the wash until January the weather will force you to delay it until February, and then you will produce varying levels of damage on peaches, pears, plums, etc.

The spring spray applied at bud burst and again at petal fall (ie, when 80% of the flowers have finished) will give you good general control of pests and, if fungicides are applied at about the same time, diseases will also be kept at bay.

Aphids are the most common pests on bush, cane fruit and strawberries, and spraying with an insecticide early in the season as the leaves open is the best plan. The currant blister aphis is always present, and prevention is better than cure in this case.

The raspberry beetle is another problem pest, but it can be controlled by spraying with liquid derris as the flowers show colour and again at 80% petal fall.

Observation and anticipation are the keys to most problems and, with the addition of a sharp knife and secateurs, a small amount of fertiliser and some pesticide and fungicide you should have plenty of fruit for the table.

Fresh strawberries from your own garden are well worth the little effort they require. The straw helps to keep the fruit clean.

A short list of recommended cultivars

Apples dessert
Ashmead Kernal, Epicure, Ellison's Orange, Egremont Russet, Cox's Orange Pippin, Laxton's Fortune, Laxton's Superb, Ribston Pippin, Worcester Pearmain.

Apples culinary
Emneth Early, George Neal, Golden Noble, Lane's Prince Albert, Monarch, Rev Wilks.

Pears
Beurre Hardy, Bristol Cross, Doyenne du Comice, Conference, Louise Bonne de Jersey, Marie Louise, Packham's Triumph.

Plums and Gages
Denniston Superb, Jefferson's Gage, Kirke's Blue, Victoria, Cambridge Gage, Coe's Golden Drop.

Damsons
Merryweather.

Apricots
Large Early, Moorpark.

Peaches
Hale's Early, Peregrine, Rochester, Royal George.

Nectarines
Lord Napier, Elruge, Pineapple.

Black Currants
Laxton's Giant, Boskoop Giant, Raven, Westwick Choice.

Red Currants
Laxton's No 1, Red Lake.

Raspberries
Malling Jewel, Malling Promise, Lloyd George.

Strawberries
Cambridge Vigour, Cambridge Favourite, Royal Sovereign.

Chapter 8
Trees & shrubs

The first thing I learned about trees was how to fell them. As a lad at school, I went on a 'forestry expedition' during the summer holidays and earned my first wage packet wielding an axe and a cross-cut saw.

I became a dab hand at 'snedding' – chopping off side branches to leave a smooth trunk. To this day, a piece missing from my forefinger bears witness to the 'skills' I picked up then.

Now, of course, it's immoral and unpatriotic to talk about cutting down trees. Those 'Plant-a-Tree in '73' and 'Plant Some More in '74' campaigns taught us all about the need to supplement our arboreal resources. And even if a disappointing number of the trees we did plant promptly died through lack of proper attention, I'm sure most of us did learn more about our natural heritage.

Patience, for one thing. It's no use spraying the oak and the ash and the walnut tree with foliar feed and expecting them to spring into majestic proportions overnight. And a friend of mine (the kind of chap beloved by garden centres, who thinks he can establish his private Wisley at the drop of a credit card) found out the hard way that trees just won't be pushed around in a hurry.

Wanting to establish a leafy screen at the end of his garden before some new houses were built, he stole out into the forests of the night and uprooted some mature, 15-foot-high firs and 'transplanted' them. They repaid his vandalism, and his impatience, by leaving him with half-a-dozen very large, very dead trees to dispose of.

My own biggest problem with trees has come from a sycamore in front of the house. The tree itself is fine, but what on earth am I to do with its seedlings? They pop up all over the place and I've still failed to find a way to root them out. (I've heard it said that, if we were to abandon our countryside to nature, in the course of time the land would be one vast sycamore forest, stifling every other plant and tree. I'm rather worried about that happening in my own garden.)

Foreign travel and long hot summers in recent years have had another effect on our national tree-growing habits: there's been a tremendous upsurge in the cultivation of tropical palms.

In my *Garden News* column I told the story of a certain Max Oliver-Davis from the London borough of Enfield who wanted to start a great campaign to grow more palms. He claimed that he was 'refuting our so-called awful' weather and he seemed to be proving his point.

In his own front garden he had five Cordyline indivisa and australis, one Trachycarpus fortuneii and four eucalyptus. He also had five fig trees grown from cuttings and a house plant ivy, Hedera canariensis.

The Cordylines were grown from seed, kept in the greenhouse in pots throughout each winter and then planted out in the pots each summer until they were mature enough to be planted permanently. After six winters outside, they stood about 9 feet high.

The eucalyptus (which can only be grown from seed) had grown to 26 feet just three years after being planted out.

However, it's too much of a tall order for most people to grow trees in modern postage-stamp gardens. Shrubs are in much greater demand – and immensely more varied.

For me, one of the delights of shrubs is that, with so many winter-flowering varieties available, they can ensure colour in the garden for an unbroken twelvemonth.

That's provided, of course, they're well-fed, well-placed in sunny or shady positions according to their needs, properly fed, skilfully pruned, protected from pests and diseases, divided and re-planted where necessary, and so on.

Yes, well . . .

GEOFF AMOS:
'Patience is <u>the</u> virtue'

Patience is the one thing the would-be gardener must acquire, whether he's growing oak trees or mustard and cress. Even the youngster with a bit of wet flannel must learn to wait three or four days to sow his mustard if he wants it at the same time as his cress.

There has to be patience with everything, not only to wait for things to grow, but in preparing the places for them, and even in planning before you start.

Classic examples of not giving enough thought when planting which, after all, is nothing but impatience, exist in gardens almost everywhere you look. The fantastically beautiful Japanese cherry with the big rich-pink double flowers (Prunus hizakura in the books but Kanzan to most people) is often seen almost overwhelming the whole of a small front garden, and sometimes even the house as well.

Who could be blamed for falling for such a tree? An unfailing mass of blossoms every year, a naturally shapely tree needing no training or pruning, even the leaves are a good bronzy green. But a word from almost anyone in the business would be a warning against Kanzan in a small garden. Marvellous for town hall squares and the like, but listed alongside in any catalogue will be a dozen more suitable for a small garden, ranging from Ama-na-Gowa which grows into a straight-up column never more than a yard wide, to Cheal's Weeper which trails to the ground better than any weeping willow ever did. Prunus incisa is magnificent, and there's even one that flowers in the winter – Prunus subhirtella autumnalis. And, talking of weeping willows, beware, whatever you do, of the

one known as the Golden Weeper. It'll have you out of the house in a few years if you plant it too close.

And don't be fooled into thinking that you don't have to worry about a tree getting too big because you think you'll be dead and gone anyway. The times I've heard that! If you want a tree in a hurry, and most folk do, it has to be remembered that most things that grow quickly grow big. They don't just conveniently stop growing when they're the size you want them. And continuous pruning isn't the answer either. You might be able to cut round the bottom, but who's going to reach up into the top? Far better to buy a slower grower and make a fuss of it. Prepare for it well, plant it well, and look after it well so that it grows as fast as possible in the early years, and slows up later.

My choices for a specimen tree, apart from conifers, would be from Acer negundo elegantissimum, a maple with pale green and

Conifers in their various shapes, sizes and colours are a must for the garden and give good foliage colour all the year round.

yellow leaves, Betula pendula youngii, a weeping silver birch, a purple beech, a laburnum (the one with the longest and best 'chains' is vossii), and a gleditschia by the name of Sunburst. And note that only one of these has any flowers. That's because I hate sweeping up falling petals, and/or pulling up seedlings in the spring. Laburnums *do* pop up you'll say. But not vossii because it's a hybrid and doesn't make seeds, and anyway, the sight of a 'golden chain' at its best excuses everything for me.

Planting eucalyptus trees and the like is another form of impatience that rarely pays. Oh yes, they'll grow like mad. I've had Eucalyptus gunnii 20 feet high in three years in the cold East Midlands – a dozen of them. But where are they now? Well one winter I lost the lot, cut to the ground by a cold spell in January. And this is typical unless you live in Bournemouth or points due west, or unless the Gulf Stream runs into your back yard. Gunnii is the hardiest of all these grey-green expresses, but in most places one year in seven is too cold for them.

Of course, there's an excuse for being impatient if it's a screen you're after. Whether it's to stop someone looking in, or to block your view looking out, it's got to be quick or you might as well not have it at all. And it's got to be evergreen too, which limits the choice a lot. You don't have to think and study the catalogues very long for this. You plant one of the Berberis (preferably stenophylla), an Escallonia if you live by the seaside, or you really lash out and buy pot-grown Cupressus leylandii, the biggest you can afford, and you look after them with your life almost. You trim along the top when they've reached the height you want them and, believe me, that won't be long.

When buying a cotoneaster be sure you know its characteristics. Three distinct varieties are (from left to right) the free-standing bush type; the herringbone form for growing against walls and fences; and the horizontal version for ground cover.

The boys who cater for our gardening needs have really cottoned on to this 'can't wait' craze that has taken over in the last 15 or 20 years. It used to be that you planted trees in the autumn or winter or not at all. But container growing has changed all that. The principle of growing small plants in pots for easy transplanting is as old as the hills of course, but not trees – not trees 8 or 10 feet high, anyway, and in full leaf or flower. But you can choose them, cart them off, plant them, and be sat under them in a deck chair on your own lawn in a couple of hours these days. There are risks of course. They need a bit of extra care for a year or two, and the bigger they are the bigger the risk. But they're more than just a gimmick to sell stuff, contrary to the opinions of some of the older sons of the soil.

Being able to see how the thing will look immediately before you buy it, being able to plant it and enjoy it immediately, has attracted a lot of people into growing plants they would never otherwise have bothered with. And who wouldn't rather garden when the sun's shining than when you're up to your neck in mud and with a perishing cold wind blowing up the back of your jacket? I suppose I could be called one of the old school, but this instant gardening is one of these 'new fangled' ideas that I'm all in favour of.

You only have to look at the permanent things of the average garden planted 30 or 40 years ago, to realise what a change there has been in the type of plants used. 'Shrubberies' they used to call these collections. Dark, unexciting clumps of laurel – spotted if they were adventurous enough – hollies, yews, privets, and, in a fit of enthusiasm, sometimes a lilac or a mock orange blossom. They were planted possibly because they were thought to be labour saving, or where they thought nothing interesting would grow. And the garden proper was somewhere else.

But then it happened that gardens had *got* to be labour-saving anyway, and why not have beauty and colour at the same time if possible? And it is possible. Decorative shrubs, flowering and non-flowering, can be chosen

for any purpose, any soil and any situation. But, as I say, you have to *choose* them. If you don't go to any more trouble than ordering a 'dozen mixed shrubs, our selection', you'll get from the nurseryman what he wants to sell and nothing more. But if you study form a bit, look up the best things for the place, taking everything into consideration, and give him some names – real names – it will be worth your while.

Beware, particularly, of being offered things 'just as good'. That often means I haven't got what you want, but I'm not going to let you get away,' and if you aren't careful you're landed with just a 'shrubbery'. Be choosey. Keep your eyes open for things you like. Find out their names and whether they're likely to grow in your garden. And, above all, be patient.

The thing that decides what you can plant in this line, more than anything else, is whether your soil is acid or alkaline, whether in fact there's lime in it or not. But, funnily enough, shrubs aren't divided into those that like one thing and those that like the other. They are divided into those that *must* have acid soil, and those that don't mind acid or limey, which is a different thing. It means that if you've got an acid soil you can grow almost anything. If you're limey, your choice is more limited. (See chapter on composts and fertilisers.)

The importance of the ultimate size of what you plant has already been touched on with trees. But shrubs, too, can easily outgrow their positions and become a nuisance. The smaller the garden, the more you must choose carefully. Some things can be kept to size by cutting and trimming, in fact they may demand it. Brooms, for instance, should be sheared back every year after flowering. But with rhododendrons, cutting them at all is murder. This doesn't mean to say you shouldn't plant rhododendrons, because there are some that grow only a few inches high.

Remember that there are nearly always different varieties of the same shrub, that have different growing characteristics. Take cotoneasters as an example. Cotoneaster cornubia will make a tree 20 feet high. Simonsii becomes a bush 10 feet by 10 feet if left to itself, but can be clipped to make a fine hedge. The well-known Cotoneaster horizontalis grows flat against a wall like a herring-bone quite naturally. And microphyllus crawls along the ground never more than a few inches high, and will keep weeds down better than almost anything: all cotoneasters.

Clematis makes an ideal wall cover. It is best trained up a support standing about an inch from the wall to allow for circulation of air.

But look how wrong you can be if you don't get the right one.

Another important point with shrubs is to try to provide interest for as long as possible. This can be done, again, by growing different varieties of the same thing. You can have heathers in flower every day of the year with a good selection. Or you can have a large number of different things, ranging from Mahonia bealeii in January to the hydrangeas in October. In a small garden you have to compromise by using shrubs that have good shape and form all the time, and bright-coloured conifers of different habits seem to fill this bill. You may have shrubs that have colour, in leaf or flower, for a long period, such as the Japanese acers, the potentillas, or the darleyensis heathers. Or you might settle for something that you can glory in for a short time, look back on with pride, and for the rest of the year be content to look forward to with anticipation. Magnolias and brooms, forsythias and philadelphus, and, of course, rhododendrons and azaleas come into this category. With a garden that's any bigger at all than the proverbial postage stamp, you can have a touch of them all.

There are shrubs for all positions. Some will do in full shade (skimmias and mahonias); some prefer partial shade (rhododendron and azaleas); some must have open sunny places (cistus and brooms); some like it wet (bamboos and hydrangeas); hebes and lavenders like it dry; some will climb walls of their own accord (ampelopsis ivies and climbing hydrangeas); some twist round pergolas (like honeysuckles and clematis); and some will carpet the ground (periwinkles and heathers),

giving weeds no chance at all. Some are ever-green and some are not, and that has to be determined for sure. And some will stand a colder climate than others.

The business of climate is one of the reasons why we put some shrubs against walls. Sometimes we want to hide the wall above all else, and then it's a pyracantha more often than not, which is the best of the ever-greens for this purpose. But sometimes we use the wall to help the shrub. Walls hold

Few trees have more striking bark than the snake–barked maple, always a centre of attraction in the garden.

warmth, and things like Ceanothus, one of the few blue-flowering shrubs, will live happily facing south, whereas it would be winter-killed in the open. The same applies to the pink- and green-leaved Actinidia, and the sweet-smelling pineapple broom, Cytisus battandeirii. Camellias appreciate a north wall where the early morning sun can't get to the frozen buds and blooms and spoil them. And things like roses, jasmine, clematis, honeysuckle and wisteria have growth that can be trained and adapted to fit walls, fences or posts.

The most important operation in the life of a tree or shrub is when it is planted in its final position. Preparation of the ground must be thorough and, if possible, done well in advance. This allows for natural settling and the partial breaking down of the plant foods that should always be provided. The type of soil will affect the type of preparation. Ground with a heavy sub-soil must be double dug by taking the top spit off, forking up the second spit and putting in farmyard manure, compost or peat. Then replace the top soil and mix in with it peat, leaf mould or a special shrub-planting mixture, which is generally peat and fertiliser combined.

On lighter soils single digging is generally enough, still dressing the top soil, but not using fresh farmyard manure which may damage young roots. The area prepared should always be half as big again at least as the spread of the roots. Just to dig a hole, which is a great temptation with container-grown plants, is often only creating a sump where water will gather, and very likely drown the plant.

There are some rules about planting that apply whether you are doing it in the 'old fashioned' months of October, November, March or April, or in the modern way when things are growing. First the depth. Never plant anything more than two inches deeper than it was in the nursery. The soil mark on the stem is the guide, or the top of the soil level if it's a plant in a pot. Always provide a stake and a tie or two immediately for things that need it – like standard trees or shrubs with heavy tops. And knock the stake into the bottom of the hole before you fill in or you may damage precious roots.

Always fill in carefully and a little at a time, making sure all the spaces are filled. And tread firm as you fill in so that soil is in close contact with the roots. Always water in with a bucket or two of water per plant and keep on watering through the first summer anything planted after Christmas. And finally – not a rule but a recommendation – a mulch of manure, compost, leaves, or peat applied over the whole root area at least three inches thick every year in February or March is the best thing that I know of for the well-being of trees or shrubs.

Make a good job of the planting and it will save a lot of heartache later on. Left: firm the soil around dwarf conifers to establish good contact between earth and roots. Centre and right: with trees use a compost bedding in the hole for nourishment. Work in the soil between the evenly spaced roots when re-filling.

If you have an acid soil then azaleas are a must. These prolific flowering shrubs can also be grown in tubs on patios.

Chapter 9
Pools

As a handyman, I'm the only known specimen of anthropoid with five thumbs. My family have never let me forget the day I tried to change a light bulb and ended up with a hole in the ceiling through which two bare wires protruded.

That being so, I've never dared to do anything quite so adventurous as building a pond in my garden. However, it seems that I don't know what I'm missing.

Thus: 'There's nothing like a pond for transforming a garden. The beauty of lilies, the movement of gleaming fish, the reflections of sky and cloud on the water surface, all combine to give the garden a very special quality.

'And it's not only a delight to the eye. The murmuring splash of fountains, the chuckle of a waterfall and the plop of rising fish are sounds that soothe and refresh the spirit, making the water garden a haven of relaxation and retreat from the vexations of the world outside.'

No, that's not a quote from Patience Strong but from, would you believe it, a pools catalogue. They almost persuade me that I should put in 'no more than a week-end's work' to create my idyllic pond.

Let's see now. The first thing I need to do, clearly, is to dig a hole. That sounds rather hard work, but I'm going to take the advice of a friend who says that 18 inches is quite deep enough. That way, he says, the water will heat up much more quickly in the summer and the plants will therefore flourish faster. Sounds as good an excuse as any for not digging too much.

But what am I going to line the pool with? Concrete, plastic sheeting, or glass fibre? The plastic seems the easiest, but I'm not so sure whether it will have the same lasting qualities – and, being me, I can see it getting torn quite easily as I wrestle with it over the stones in the earth.

Concrete sounds the most lasting, but it also sounds a back-breaking job. Glass fibre, then? Well, I'm not so sure I have the skill to dig a hole to match the weird shapes these pools require.

Assuming (and it's a large assumption) that I manage to construct a pool, what am I going to put in it? Lilies, surely, for a start.

I'm told that planting in containers is now the most popular method, but is it the best? How else might I plant lilies – and how do I choose between the Marliacea and the other, tuberous-rooted varieties?

Having a swimming pool at home, I have learned a thing or two about algae. I've never seen anybody adding chlorine to a garden pond, so presumably I'll need to stock the pond with oxygenating plants to ensure clear water. But again – what are the best varieties and how should they be planted?

I must have some fish, of course, to eat up the insects. (It's beginning to sound like that Burl Ives' song about swallowing a spider to catch a fly, or the cycle of life on Ilkley Moor.)

Cambridge Blue Shubunkins. Yes, I simply must have some of those. At this stage, if I ever reach it, I shall be past taking advice. I shall simply choose my fish the way I pick racehorses – because I like their names.

Gleaming Golden Orfe. Calico fantail. Blue bitterling. Higoi golden carp. They're all for me.

The only thing that puts me off the whole enterprise is that apparently I must also stock the pond with snails. And even if they're called Black Ramshorns (or Palnorbis Corneus) I still don't like snails.

Must I have them to clean up the vegetable matter at the bottom of the pond? Can't I clean it up myself?

Please?

GEOFF HAMILTON:
'You won't finish it in a weekend'

Michael Barratt, you're not being fair. How can you expect lucid and practical answers to your questions when I am choked with emotion over your lyricism? Whoever wrote that piece in the pools catalogue wasn't all that far wrong, however. A pool will certainly add a wider interest to the garden and is invariably a most pleasing feature.

I'm afraid I have bad news for you though. Unless you have the industry of a beaver, the stamina of a marathon runner and a set of arc lights, you won't finish it in a weekend.

Before you rush out with wildly flailing spade, you really should consider the design of the pool.

The correct site is of paramount importance. In a small garden, for example, the pool is likely to be the most eye-catching feature, so it must be sited in a spot where it will complement rather than detract from the rest of the scheme. You may well prefer still water that will reflect some striking feature – or you may use it as an integral part of a rockery.

A sunny spot will improve the growth of aquatic plants, though it will increase the incidence of algae. These should not present a great problem if you shade the surface of the water with lilies. Much more of a nuisance are trees, which will fill the pool with fallen leaves in the autumn, so keep well clear of them.

Depth in relation to surface area is important. Certainly, no pool should be less than 15 inches deep, and it is never necessary to go down more than 3 feet. As a rule of thumb method, you can say that a pool of less than 100 sq ft in surface area need not be deeper than 18 inches, from 100 sq ft to 300 sq ft a depth of 2 feet is desirable, and over that it is worth the effort to excavate to 3 feet.

If you intend to grow marginal plants as well as deep water subjects, you'll need some shelves. Since marginals like to have a couple of inches of water over their roots, the shelves should be about 9 inches deep. This will allow for the depth of the planting pot, plus that 2 inches of water.

Right. Now you have dug the hole to the correct depth and you've incorporated the shelves, the worst is over. The rest is all fun.

Without doubt, the easiest way to build a pool is with a liner. Concrete is backbreaking, difficult and costly and, worse still, it's pretty difficult to make a good job of it.

There are basically three types of liner, the cheapest of which is polythene. Like everything else, I'm afraid, you get what you pay for, and the snag with polythene is that it won't last overlong. The action of sunlight and soil bacteria will degrade it in a fairly short time.

Much higher in my list of preferences comes reinforced PVC which will give you a much longer-lasting pool than polythene.

If you can afford a swimming pool in your back garden, you can afford a butyl rubber liner, and it's well worth the extra cost. Here is a really strong material that will be affected neither by sunlight nor by bacteria. First developed for large-scale projects such as reservoirs, butyl will last at least 50 years, and probably upwards of 100.

Glass fibre and pre-formed plastic pools are simplicity itself to install but, as well as the high cost of glass fibre, have the disadvantage that you are stuck with a particular design – and some of the designs are quite useless for fish and plants.

Having decided upon the material to use, let me put your mind at rest on the traumas of construction.

Water, of course, always finds a perfect level. So, to avoid having a foot of unsightly wall showing at one side of the pool, it is important to get the finished levels right. The easiest way I have found is to use a series of pegs, a straight edge and a spirit level. Put the pegs all round the perimeter of the pool, having first marked a clear line 4 inches below the top of the peg. Using the straight edge and spirit level, set the pegs exactly level. Now excavate so that the finished level of the rim of the pool coincides with the marks on the

pegs. This way, the water will come right to the top all round and the liner will be hidden. Remove the pegs before installing the liner. The method of fitting a liner is exactly the same whichever material you use.

You were quite right about those stones. Plastic is a pretty tough material, and butyl-rubber even tougher, but both will cut easily with a sharp edge. Small stones make a quick and efficient job of it. To avoid this, the bottom and sides of the pools must be covered first with a couple of inches of soft sand or sieved earth. If your pool has steep sides, use layers of wet newspaper.

Stretch the liner over the top of the hole and anchor it with a few stones, or a shovelful of

Stages in the construction of a liner pool: excavate the hole, allowing for a shelf to take marginal water plants; position the liner, holding it in place with a few bricks or stones; and complete by edging the pool with stone and filling it with water.

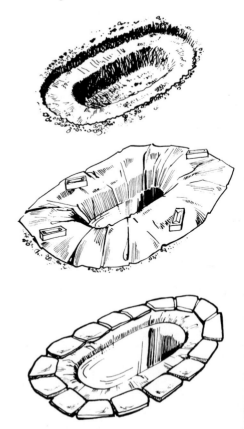

soil at the appropriate places.

Now simply fill up with water. The weight of the water will push the liner down until it fits snugly into the hole. Obviously, as the liner settles, creases will appear in places, and these should be neatly folded over.

When the pool is completely full, trim off the edges of the liner, leaving about 6 inches all round.

The job is completed by either paving or turfing around the outside, over the cut edges of the liner.

Glass fibre and pre-formed plastic pools are, if anything, even easier. First of all, measure the rough size of the pool, and dig the hole a little larger. Set the pool in the hole and, with a spirit level and straight edge, check for level both ways. The outside of the hole can now be refilled with fine soil, ramming it well home under the pool. Again, finish off by paving or turfing around the edge.

Though some gardeners may like a still pool that will reflect the trees and the sky, my own preference is for moving water. This can take the form of a fountain, a waterfall, or, for the very ambitious, even a stream.

The choice will depend primarily upon the design of the pool. I feel that the shape should be informal for a waterfall, and formal for a fountain. I know a lot of people have both fountain and waterfall. Well, I suppose, one man's meat is another man's poison, but to me, they look pretty incongruous.

Whichever you decide upon, you will need a pump to circulate the water. Basically, there are two types, surface pumps and submersible. A surface pump remains outside the pool, while the submersible type drops into the water.

Surface pumps have the advantage that there is practically no limit to their size. So, for the really large pool, you may have to plump for one of these. However, for the amateur, submersible pumps are very much easier to install, and therefore to be preferred.

Messing about with electricity is against my religion – I'm a devout coward – so this is the one thing I would suggest you get a tradesman to do for you.

A pool without plants and fish is like chips without vinegar – but that's a big subject. Your best bet, as with planting a new garden, is to start with a basic collection, to which you will want to add as you learn more.

Lilies are a must. Not only are they the most exotic plants in the pool, but they also provide shade for the water. This is important in the fight against algae.

The marliacea group are perhaps the easiest to grow, vigorous, very hardy and, incidentally, scented (though how you get your nose to the middle of the pool, I have never discovered). Of these, the most popular is the large, white-flowered, Nymphaea marliacea albida. This, like others in the group, will grow in water 10 - 24 inches above the crown. One of my favourites is Nymphaea marliacea chromatella, with its soft yellow blooms and mottled foliage. It's very free flowering (given a sunny spot), and is suitable for a medium-sized pool.

For a fairly large pool, Nymphaea attraction is not to be missed. It is pretty vigorous, with large leaves and big, red flowers. Of the lilies for smaller pools, or the shallower parts of large ones, I would go for Nymphaea pygmaea helvola, a delightful plant with tiny, mottled leaves and lots of pale yellow flowers, and Nymphaea pygmaea alba. This has rather larger leaves and, as the name suggests, white flowers.

Planting lilies, and indeed all aquatic plants, is generally done in plastic or wire containers these days. This method is certainly the most convenient, and the restriction of the roots does tend to reduce the amount of leaf the plant will make. This is, of course, a good

Water lilies go at the bottom of a pool in containers. Marginal plants are situated in the shallower portions, while aerating greenery is either weighted to the bottom or floats at the surface.

Sectional view of a concrete pool showing humus covered with washed gravel and the lipped shelves.

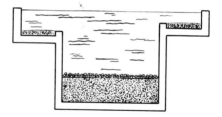

thing in most pools, and it doesn't seem to effect the amount of flower the plant will produce. You certainly can plant in a layer of soil on the bottom of the pool, and this will give more vigorous growth – but it's a lot of trouble.

When you buy the roots, they will probably have been cut back. If not, do so quite severely. Plant in sterilised loam, with the crown just above the surface. Ram the soil very firmly around the root, and finish off with a layer of washed gravel. This will help to stop the soil floating out of the container and clouding the water.

One word of warning. Don't lower the container to the bottom of the pool straight away. Put a few bricks in the water so that when the container rests on them the lily leaves are no more than an inch or so below the surface.

After about a week, the plant can be lowered a little more, and so on until it's on the bottom.

Water hawthorn is another good choice for planting on the bottom. This has pure white flowers with jet black anthers, is very free flowering over a long period, and will grow in any depth from 4 to 18 inches.

Floating plants are just about the easiest thing in the world to plant – just chuck 'em in. However, most of them are rampant growers, so be prepared for a clear-out every so often. Fairy moss (Azolla caroliniana) forms a carpet of green that later changes to a beautiful

Alternative method of producing a liner pool, utilising rocks to conceal the top portion but providing a number of small shelves for container plants. The extra bottom liner is a safeguard against damage.

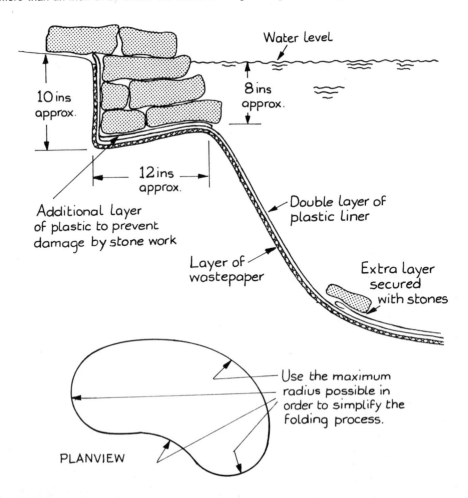

Water level

10 ins approx.

8 ins approx.

12 ins approx.

Additional layer of plastic to prevent damage by stone work

Double layer of plastic liner

Layer of wastepaper

Extra layer secured with stones

Use the maximum radius possible in order to simplify the folding process.

PLANVIEW

red, and Frog-bit (Hydrocharis morsus-ranae) looks like a tiny lily, with prolific, white flowers.

Of the hundreds of marginal plants available, I would start with Caltha palustris plena, the double marsh marigold, whose double yellow flowers make a bright splash throughout April and May, a few of the varieties of Iris laevigata, and the bright yellow of Mimulus guttatus.

All these can be planted in pots on the pool shelves so that they are covered with just an inch or two of water.

The initial collection should be finished off with a few oxygenating plants, to provide essential oxygen for fish. The best bet here is to buy a collection. They are generally sold bunched and weighted, so planting consists of simply throwing them in. They are rampant growers, so may need clearing out after a while.

Of all the fish available, my advice is to stick to the humble goldfish. They are the most colourful of all and, most important, they feed near the top, so you can see them. Later on you may want to try a few shubunkins, Golden Orfe or Fantails but, for all but the fish fanatic, goldfish will give the most colour and the least trouble.

Snails? No, I don't think they're essential at all. True, they do a bit of cleaning up here and there, but some also attack aquatic plants and though they may possibly, on balance, do slightly more good than harm, I wouldn't bother.

You certainly do have a point about algae. But, generally, the best cure is patience and philosophy. Algae thrive on sunlight, carbon dioxide, mineral salts and warmth. New pools have all these ingredients in abundance: fresh soil in plant containers provides mineral salts, and the plants have not made enough growth to shade the pool. So within a few days of planting, the water will inevitably go like pea soup. Don't clear it all out and start again because they'll come back every time. Instead, just leave it and the algae will eventually disappear. You won't ever get rid of it all, though – and this is, in fact, a very happy state of affairs for the fish and plants. So, use a bit of your renowned north-country philosophy, and learn to live with it!

Chapter 10
Bedding plants & borders

Gardeners, of course, are old-fashioned folk. They're unwilling to move with the times. They don't like innovation. Their roots are in the soil and that's where they're going to stay.

Of course?

I'm not so sure. Apart from the obvious revolution in amateur gardeners' techniques brought about by the development of chemical fertilisers, fungicides, pesticides, insecticides and all the rest; apart from the increasing mechanisation that's to be observed on even small plots, gardeners follow fashion as much as well-dressed women. Well, almost as much.

Consider, for example, the case of one of the oldest horticultural societies in the land. (Patron, Her Majesty the Queen; President, due to some strange mental aberration on the part of the members, me.)

It began life 75 years ago as the Windsor Chrysanthemum Society and by all accounts it flourished – until a trend developed for the growing of dahlias and many members began to drift away.

Moving with the times, the name was changed to the Windsor Chrysanthemum and Dahlia Society. But once more gardening fashions overtook them, so the name had to be changed yet again.

Today, they've had to add the words 'and Horticultural' to their title – and you can be sure that the largest number of entries for their annual show will be from fuchsia growers. For the moment, that is. Who can tell what the next fad will be?

Similarly, I've noticed a great upsurge recently in the growing of herbs. It's a trend I deplore because it goes with a nasty tendency to use things like Rosemary and Basil for cooking nowadays, which ruins good wholesome food.

In the garden, though, there's a lot to be said for the use of herbs either in a small area on their own – a collection of plants like Borage, Chervil, Fennel, Marjoram, Dill, Tarragon, and so on can be a delight to the eye – or as border plants.

The feathered leaves and white flowers of Caraway, for instance, can add pleasing variety among bedding plants; Parsley and Thyme make attractive borders.

But perhaps the most way-out trend recently has been the growing practice of talking to plants.

At the very least, it's likely that those who care enough about their flowers to talk to them will handle them with a kind of tenderness that's bound to produce better results.

I never met a successful gardener yet who didn't care in some special way for the things he grew.

It must be said, too, that no less a person than that great philosopher, Dr Albert Schweitzer, believed passionately throughout his long life that plants have what we'd call a 'soul' just like the rest of us.

That's why he believed it was sinful even to pick a wild flower in the field. That, he said, was 'careless pleasure'. It meant taking life instead of revering it.

My own attitude to flowers is much more down-to-earth. I simply want to grow them in profusion, trying to ensure plenty of bright colours in my garden for as many months of the year as possible. To that end, I want to know more about the choice available to me and the best methods of bedding out hardy and half-hardy annuals, perennials and biennials.

I'm particularly attracted to some of the new F1 hybrids in the glossy catalogues, though I'm not sure what 'F1' means. I've tried asking the flowers themselves but they remain stubbornly uncommunicative . . .

GEOFF AMOS:
'Combine plants and design'

The British climate prevents us keeping our gardens equally colourful and smart all the year round, but no one expects the same level of attraction anyway, and I doubt if anyone really wants it. After all, we should never appreciate the beauties of spring and summer if there were no dull and dark months. But there's no reason why we shouldn't drastically shorten the 'off' period by choosing the right plants.

Summer's easy, of course. Half-a-dozen roses, a few boxes of bedding plants, a dahlia or two and you'll have the colour, even if you don't win any prizes for garden design. And, if there's no early frost, these basics will take care of the autumn as well. Spring presents no problem: although your early show needs planning the year before (because that's when you plant it), it's only a case of remembering to get in some wallflowers, polyanthus and bulbs before the bad weather starts.

But there are many plants that will prolong the autumn season, and another lot that will hurry on the spring. There are some that will even brighten the middle of winter, whatever the weather. And growing as many (and as varied a selection) as possible from these is the secret of having an all-the-year-round garden.

It depends to some extent on what sort of a person you are as to whether or not you're successful at all-year gardening. If, for instance, you're one of those tidy minded creatures who, as soon as the first touch of frost has blackened a leaf or two in September, feels compelled to clear everything out to the compost heap, lock, stock and aster, and digs up every inch of ground so that everything's 'fresh', as it's called – well, you'll have a year-round garden all right, spick and span, but not a fraction of the colour you could have.

And if you're the opposite, a somewhat reluctant gardener who fills the ground with 'permanent' plants and then never does another thing to them but sit back and watch them grow – well, you'll probably get your spring, summer, autumn and winter show for a year or two. But soon the old order of the survival of the fittest begins to operate, and it isn't long before your garden's taken over by the strong. The weak, generally the things you like most, have gone to the wall.

Then there's the middle way, for the in-between sort of gardener which most of us are. This means using some permanent plants to make a backbone, or a framework, and having areas between where we can 'garden' away to our heart's content. The sizes of these areas will depend on how keen we are or how much time we want to spend. In them we can plant our fancies and our favourites.

A lawn is almost certain to be on everyone's list, and maybe a lawn completely surrounded by permanent plants will satisfy you, and the work of mowing the lawn and pruning and trimming the shrubs could be all you want to have to cope with. Perhaps, however, beds cut into the lawn and filled with roses is your ideal. For the more ambitious, areas filled twice a year with bedding plants will certainly give maximum colour for six or seven out of the 12 months.

On the other hand, it may be that you want to spend your gardening time in growing chrysanthemums, dahlias or sweet peas for showing. These have to be grown in rows, so that they can be attended to with all the fads and frills the showman lavishes on them. But it is almost impossible to incorporate their beauty into the scheme of a show garden and they have to be kept apart, generally grown in the vegetable patch or, to most wives' disgust, in place of it.

When planting out half-hardy plants into their flowering positions, ease a few at a time from the seed tray and separate them on a sheet of paper. Plant them 9 inches apart.

Asters make a good subject for grouping arrangements.

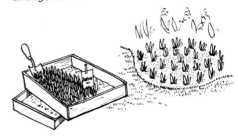

A rockery and a pool may enter into your scheme of things, or perhaps even a completely paved garden, with tubs and troughs filled with suitable subjects. Whichever you choose, you have to accept that the beauty in winter will come in a subdued form, in shapes and shades rather than colour, and it must come from permanent plants.

These, then, are the ones to plant in the borders in strategic places, where they can be seen from the house in winter. They must be evergreen in the main, and for a start I would look no further than the lovely garden conifers, choosing Cupressus donard gold or Chamaecyparis stewartii for upright positions, and one of the many junipers for spread. When it comes to a small standard tree to stand out on its own, the berried Cotoneaster pendula or the deciduous but

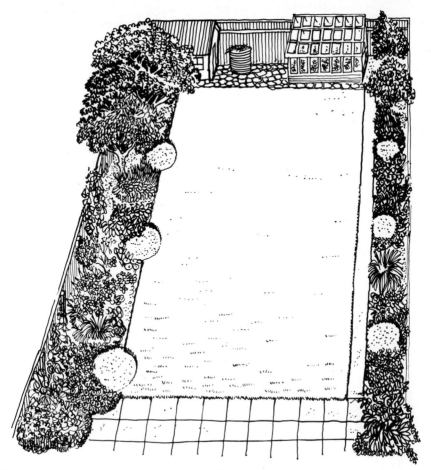

beautiful snake-bark acer are ideal.

For winter flowers, plant heathers in two or three varieties that will give colour from November until April. Between and around these (if your soil is acid), rhododendrons and camellias will give 'body' with their polished winter leaves. Berberis and skimmias will do in shady places, while Eleagnus aurea varie- gata give a grand splash of yellow, Senecio of grey, and Euonymous variegata of silver and cream. In a sheltered spot the polished leaves of Choisya, the Mexican orange blos- som, look well, and I would never despise a good form of the spotted laurel, Aucuba, especially in a town garden.

Attraction early in the year can come from a Daphne mezereum, the yellow-leaved Philadelphus 'aureum', or Magnolia stellata, and late in the year from the many subjects that give berries or good autumn leaf colour.

The spaces between these backbone plants

Plan of a small garden showing permanent and semi-permanent plants with spaces left for twice-yearly bedding out.

can be filled in many different ways. For example, additional shrubs in a variety of form and colour can be made to cover the ground completely, suppressing weed growth and only needing judicious trimming and pruning to keep them from stifling each other.

Roses are glorious in summer, but thorny nuisances the rest of the year. Herbaceous plants are permanent and labour-saving, but at the same time will satisfy the chap who likes something to do now and again, because they have to be pruned every year and split up and re-planted every three or four years. But our famous – or infamous – twice- a-year bedding-out system, despite the work and expense involved, will give more bright colour in the garden than anything else.

In theory you can combine all these alternatives but in practice it doesn't work too well. You curse the rose thorns, because you're apt to forget they are there; you disturb roots you shouldn't touch when you dig up and divide great slabs of herbaceous plants; and bedding plants tend to look spotty if they're just put around in ones and twos in the gaps.

It is better by far to make each space between your 'permanents' a feature on its own, taking the size and shape into account. Not only is this a more convenient way of gardening, but you can also cater for the special requirements of a particular group of plants. If a group of roses is planned, for instance, they are semi-permanents and need good ground preparation that will last them for several years. The top spit is taken off, the bottom broken up and plenty of manure or compost worked in, then the top, mixed with peat or leaf-mould and rose fertiliser, is replaced. Roses must also have full light. If they have to compete with other, smothering plants around them, they grow up thin and drawn with poor flowers on the top of long, ugly and bare stems.

Most herbaceous plants, on the other hand, are more surface rooting. They need humus and fertiliser in the top layers of soil, and room between them for the roots to spread. They want a mulch to keep them moist through the summer and, above all, they need open space around them in the spring, because if their new growths are hampered in any way they, too, grow thin and weak, unable to stand up or carry the flower heads.

Bedding plants need ground that is easily worked in both winter and summer. It never has time to lie fallow for the weather to break it up, but it must be in workable and plantable condition both in October and in May. Never tread on beds when they're wet, because this destroys the essential planting texture quicker than anything else. The soil needs peat and sand in the top few inches so that it will break up with a light forking and can be Dutch-hoed easily to kill the inevitable seedling weeds. And use quick-acting fertilisers from a bag rather than great slabs of farmyard manure that the ground will take some time to digest.

So, keeping the garden colourful over as many months of the year as possible needs a combination of plants and design. The absolute essentials are the permanents which will provide the attraction in winter, placed in positions carefully worked out with the overall picture in mind. These are always trees

No border would be complete without a bank of marigolds, providing a succession of flowers for the best part of the summer. These are dwarf varieties that can be planted out in May.

and/or shrubs. The spaces between them, whatever size and shape, will be filled in with either more permanents (shrubs of different shapes, sizes and colours, flowering and non-flowering, but chosen to give as much colour as possible over as long a period as possible), semi-permanents (roses and herbaceous plants), or non-permanent twice-a-year bedding plants.

For the formal-minded gardener, the spaces can be cut and shaped in herbaceous-border style, or in beds of set designs with the 'fillers' in set groups. In an informal garden the dividing line between the walking places and the growing area will be the only formal aspect. The rest will be a mixture of every kind of plant, though this has its disadvantages, as we have seen. Formality wins the day in most cases. Beds and borders are more easily designed and looked after than areas with undefined limits, and a lesser knowledge of plants is needed.

Spring and summer bedding, though expensive to keep up if you have to buy everything ready grown, is quite economical if you grow your own plants from seed and don't count the time you spend raising them! Bulbs for the spring cost money, but if only a few are

A good example of the well-thought-out garden, mixing permanents, semi-permanents and annual plants in heights according to their position.

bought each year their numbers soon mount up. Seeds of wallflowers, forget-me-nots, polyanthus, sweet williams, canterbury bells and foxgloves cost very little, and these can all be sown outside, or in a cold frame, in March, April or May. They are then grown on to flowering size in the open garden in the summer and planted into their flowering positions in October. And nothing compares with a bed of wallflowers or polyanthus in spring, whether interplanted with bulbs or not.

As soon as they're finished out they come, and in go the summer glories: the marigolds and petunias, alyssum and lobelias, salvias and antirrhinums. These can all be raised from packets of seeds if you have a greenhouse, or you can buy them in the familiar boxes ready to plant out in May and early June.

The beauty and advantage of this twice-a-year bedding is that there is an almost endless combination of subjects in different colours and forms to choose from.

Varieties of annuals and biennials are endless, as the catalogues and seed displays show. They are added to every year, not only with new flowers from all parts of the world, but with new colours and forms of old favourites. F1 hybrid varieties have a built-in consistency of form, colour and reliability bred into them by the careful and scientific selection of their parentage along very strict lines, providing absolute control over all their characteristics. The seeds are more expensive to produce, more expensive to buy, but just as easy to grow. And you can be sure that they are improvements on ordinary varieties, not just someone's fad, as many ordinary new introductions often are.

Finally, a word about talking to plants. No doubt it helps, but I have always thought it more important to be able to listen to plants talking to you! They *do* talk – in sign language – but if you can learn to interpret their signals the art of gardening becomes an open book.

Ideas for a garden for all seasons

Permanent plants
Golden and 'blue' conifers; evergreen trees and shrubs; and trees with attractive barks for winter; winter flowering heathers in variety; shrubs with grey leaves, variegated leaves, golden leaves, autumn colours and berries; shrubs with long flowering lives (potentillas, hydrangeas, hypericums, heathers, hebes); shrubs for ground cover; bulbs for interplanting and naturalising.

Semi-permanent plants
Roses, preferably vigorous floribundas; herbaceous plants and alpines, such as alstroemeria, Alyssum saxatile, aquilegia, aubretia, bergenia, campanula, delphinium, doronicum, helenium, helianthemum, helianthus, helleborus, heuchera, hosta, irises, lupins, michaelmas daisies, paeonias, phlox, pinks, pyrethrums, saxifraga, scabious, solidago and thyme.

Bedding plants from seed
Bellis (daisies), forget-me-nots, polyanthus and wallflowers for spring flowering; canterbury bells, foxgloves and sweet williams for late spring and summer; antirrhinums, alyssum, lobelia, petunias, stocks, marigolds, salvias, nemesia, asters and dahlias for summer.

Summer flower from seeds sown direct in their flowering positions
Annual chrysanthemums, clarkia, cornflowers, eschscholzias, godetias, gypsophila, lavatera, limnanthes, love in a mist, nasturtiums and nemophila.

Asters make an ideal border flower and are available in a wide range of sizes and colours.

Chapter 11
Roses

Wandering around a large garden some time ago, my friend Bill Sowerbutts pronounced judgment on it: 'The garden is winning 2 – 1 at half time'.

I knew exactly what he meant. The scoreline is about the same in the match between my roses and me.

Most of us are tempted to think that there are few easier ways of creating a colourful garden than buying a few pounds' worth of roses at the local garden centre, planting them in beds or borders, and sitting back to enjoy their colour and fragrance. Yet there's probably more to learn about cultivating and caring for roses than about anything else in the garden.

The initial choice presents enough permutations to send you reeling – hybrid tea or floribunda, miniature or shrub, rambler or climber, and within those groups a dozen different types like half or full standard, pillar or climber, bush or dwarf bush.

Every year new varieties appear to confuse the issue still further. Peace, Mischief, Fragrant Cloud, Ohlala, Vagabonde, New Dawn, Sweet Briar, Ena Harkness, Christian Dior, Alison Wheatcroft, Josephine Bruce, Elizabeth of Glamis, Fred Loads . . .

And there's little point in reading tips on caring for your roses before a whole new language has been learned concerning sepals and stipules, suckers and snags, necks and nodes.

As my own rose beds will testify, there are almost as many pests and diseases to be controlled as there are varieties of rose. Greenfly in particular seem to have reached almost plague proportions in recent years. Black spot, mildew and rust are all too common.

What's to be done about them? Spraying with this or that proprietary insecticide is usually recommended, but I'd like to know more about what causes these things, so that I could at least attempt prevention rather than cure.

Skilful pruning seems to be the chief secret of producing really floriferous roses – and it's a skill which has so far eluded me. I do it too hard or too light, too early or too late in the season. Is there a hard and fast rule about how and when to prune, I wonder?

And what should I feed them? Some of my friends swear by mushroom humus. I got rather good results from chicken droppings mixed with wood shavings, but we no longer have poultry at home so I need a substitute.

Is foliar feeding all that it's cracked up to be?

What are the advantages of disbudding?

Should I remove dead blooms during the flowering period?

Is it a good idea to take cuttings – or should I leave that to the experts?

As I say, there's an awful lot to learn about roses.

CYRIL HARRIS:
'Dismiss the misconceptions'

Growing roses successfully is not so difficult as Michael implies. Admittedly you have to discipline yourself to do some fairly easy tasks regularly. Above all, you must dismiss the misconceptions and bogies that, over the years, have contributed to the mystique which surrounds rose growing.

Some people think that you must have clay soil to grow good roses. This is quite wrong, because they will flourish in any soil except a chalky one. Certainly they like clay, but only because it holds the moisture, and any soil can be made to do this if you add humus makers, such as peat, farmyard manure or good garden compost. If your soil is chalky, however, unless you are dedicated and prepared to devote two years to making it 'habitable', you would be wise to grow something else.

Ideally you should choose a position that is in the shade for part of the day, and the soil should be prepared by thorough digging and incorporating a humus-making material.

When it comes to planting your roses, remember they are destined to give you joy for many years; so do it well. Dig a hole large enough for the roots to be spread out and of such a depth that the union – the swollen part on the main stem a few inches above the roots – is just about level with the soil's surface. It

helps to mix a little bone meal and damp peat, blended two handfuls to one bucketful respectively, in the soil just below and above the roots.

Except for pruning and fighting diseases and pests, cultivating roses is fairly easy. Let's deal first with feeding them. They are not really gross feeders, but they like regular

First (left) and second year (right) pruning of hybrid tea and floribunda roses. The black marks indicate where the cuts should be made.

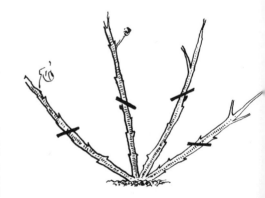

meals, and this is done in two stages. Firstly, in February, every three roses should be given two handfuls of a slow-acting organic fertiliser, such as fishmeal. This is slowly broken down, giving a steady supply of nutrients throughout the summer. In spring and summer give them a proprietary rose fertiliser at the recommended dosage level. This contains quick-acting chemicals, which will give the roses an immediate boost just when they need it.

Coupled with feeding, there must be copious watering, which is essential to the absorption of plant foods from the soil and to the processes by which the plants make their foods. Mulching over your rosebeds during May, ie, distributing a 2-3 inch layer of rotted farmyard manure, well-made garden compost, or peat, all of which are substitutes for Michael's chicken droppings and wood shavings, helps the soil to retain moisture during hot days. It is also labour-saving, because it prevents weeds. Ultimately dug in, it provides humus to condition the soil.

Quite justifiably, Michael asks: 'Is foliar feeding all that it's cracked up to be?' The answer to this pointed question is that it's no substitute for feeding with the solid fertilisers described above. It is an excellent first-aid measure to be applied in a crisis, such as failure of sap to rise during a cold spring, or as new leaves grow after loss of foliage from any cause, since it speeds up the vital food manufacturing process in the plant.

Michael suggests that to grow roses well it is necessary to be familiar with a number of names for the parts of the rose plant. This is not the case. Of those he mentions, the two that matter most are snags and suckers. Snags are the dieback that occurs when a stem is pruned or broken off high above a bud. A sharp lookout should be kept for snags and they should be removed forthwith because they may become hosts for diseases.

Now suckers are things that trouble quite a lot of gardeners, because they are never quite sure whether a new shoot growing near the ground is a guilty growth or not. With hybrid tea, floribunda and other roses grown on rootstocks there is only one criterion. Does it emerge below the union or appear through the soil from the root? If it does the latter, it is a sucker. Remove it by *tearing*, not cutting, scraping away the soil if necessary to expose its origin.

Michael asks what the advantage is of disbudding. From the standpoint of an ordinary gardener, who delights in continuous colour in his rosebeds, there is really no advantage to be gained. In any case the practice is confined to hybrid tea roses, some varieties of which produce more than one bud on each flowering stalk. It is quite obvious that when this happens, the nutrients in the sap that rises in this stem have to be shared by all the buds, and in consequence they never produce such large individual flowers. But if the stem is disbudded, ie the outer buds are

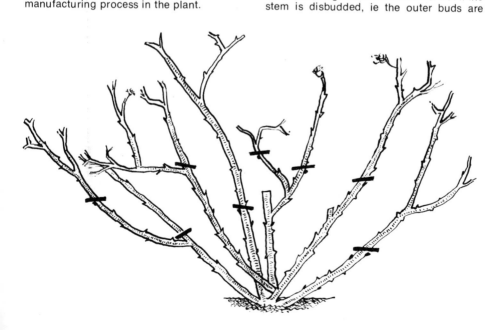

pinched out as soon as they are large enough to handle, the one remaining gets all the rations, and grows into a bumper size. Actually you can take your choice.

If you want to have one large hybrid tea bloom of excellent shape, and this is what rose exhibitors plump for, you should disbud, but if you prefer a larger number of rather smaller flowers, following one another in succession, let them go their own sweet way.

Another question that many beginners want answering is one that Michael also asks: 'Should I remove dead blooms during the flowering period?' The answer is 'Yes', particularly in the case of hybrid tea, floribunda, modern climbers and many old fashioned repeat-flowering roses, such as hybrid musks, bourbons, hybrid perpetuals and rugosas, which are still obtainable and popular these days. This is because removing the flowers as soon as they fade accelerates a new show of colourful blooms. It is not an arduous task, perhaps even a soothing one to perform in the quiet of a peaceful summer's evening at the end of a busy day.

Then, as Michael says, there are all the pests and diseases. The pests that most commonly attack our roses are grouped into two classes. Firstly there are the sap-suckers, such as the greenflies and thrips. These can be destroyed with systemic insecticides, which enter the sap and poison them. Secondly there are the leaf-eaters, such as caterpillars, which do not imbibe sufficient poisoned sap to kill them and have to be sprayed with a contact insecticide. Gardeners do not have to worry about these differences, because they can buy proprietaries which are mixtures of both types. Generally, insecticides are applied when the pests are detected and then about a month later to keep the roses out of trouble.

The most frequently encountered diseases that attack roses are due to the fungi – mildew, black spot and rust. The rest are not such serious menaces. Michael says he would like to know more about what causes these things. So would we all, including the scientists who are studying them. Despite the progress that has been made we are still a long way off solving these problems. But quite a lot of useful hints directed towards minimising the effects have come out of this work.

Most of these tips are simple things that anyone with a minimal knowledge of these diseases can carry out. The first thing to be done is to gather up as many autumn fallen leaves as possible and burn them, because it is now known that the diseases are likely to survive the winter on them and launch an attack in the following spring. Any remaining leaves should be hoed in because the spores are destroyed if covered with soil.

Particularly in the case of black spot, all affected leaves left on the bush in autumn should be picked off and burnt, because this fungus lives through the winter. More

Three common mistakes in pruning a stem, and the correct angle and position for a cut.

 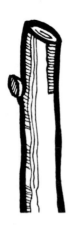  

CUT
SLOPING
WRONG
WAY

CUT
TOO
FAR
AWAY

CUT
TOO
CLOSE

CORRECT

Black spot, one of the most common rose diseases.

recently the 'boffins' have found that mildew overwinters in the first three or four top leaf buds on a stem, especially if the flower has been infected during the season. All shoots should consequently be reduced by about one-third in early December.

As arduous, and sometimes hopeless, as it might sometimes seem, spraying regularly with a fungicide does help to control these diseases. In the case of mildew and black spot, there are systemics such as Benlate and Murphy's Systemic Fungicide, which enter the tissues of the leaves and fight these menaces from within. It is wise to spray your roses every fortnight or so throughout the summer. Because these systemics get under the skin of the leaves, there is no need to re-spray if rain falls a few hours after application as they cannot be washed away. With rust, regular spraying is needed if it appears, but this time with a contact fungicide, such as Maneb, which coats the surface of the leaves. All leaves and shoots bearing the tell-tale rust or orange spots should be removed and burnt when they first appear in the spring.

Perhaps pruning is the greatest bogey to most beginners. Echoing their sentiments, Michael asks when and how this should be done. All hybrid teas and floribundas are pruned in late winter or early spring, because they bloom on the shoots that grow during the same season. For ramblers, pruning must be done during the summer, immediately after they have finished flowering, because they bloom on the shoots that were grown the previous year. The exact date when hybrid teas and floribundas should be pruned depends upon the latitude and degree of exposure of the garden. If it is in the south of England, pruning can commence in February, whereas in the north, or if it is in a very cold position, it should be postponed until late March.

Those who would appreciate some rules for pruning will be pleased to know that there are some quite helpful tips. The first is to be sure that your secateurs are always sharp to avoid crushing the shoots. The second is always to make the cut just above an outward-pointing bud, with a cut that slopes downwards from about ⅛ inch above the eye. This helps to keep the bush open in the centre so that light gets to the middle and air circulates freely. The next rule, which follows naturally, is to cut away all last year's shoots that grow in towards the centre. Finally, all weak, dead and diseased wood is removed. You then have a nice, clean, cup-shaped rose tree, composed of a number of main stems all waiting for the final operation.

Still, there are more rules. Both hybrid teas and floribundas are pruned down to three or four eyes from the ground, whichever is point-

Planting sequence for roses. Make sure that the hole is large enough to take the roots without cramping and work the soil well into them. Standard roses will need a stake and this should be driven home before the tree is planted to avoid root damage.

ing outwards, during the first spring after planting. The experts call this 'hard pruning'.

Subsequently there is a parting of the ways. The hybrid tea roses are pruned every year at an outward-growing bud, at about half length. This is termed 'moderate pruning'.

With floribundas, present-day pruning is aimed at maintaining that very lovely succession of blooms throughout the summer, which is characteristic of this type of rose. Look at your floribundas after you have removed all the unwanted wood and you will see there are two types of shoots – new green ones growing from the base and older ones branching from the stems you pruned last year. Remove flowers only from the new shoots, at the first outward-growing bud below the base of the cluster. This is known as 'light pruning'. These will flower again earlier in the season. Next, all the other shoots should be pruned back to half their length. These shoots, being more mature and more severely pruned, will bloom later, giving a glorious succession of colour.

Most climbers, other than ramblers, need little pruning beyond that necessary to keep them in shape and to size. There are, however, two types of rambler, both of which need rather more pruning. The first grows all its new shoots from near the base. As those produced in summer will give next year's flowers, all of the old shoots that have flowered are cut away at a point only a few inches from the ground. The second type of rambler produces new wood higher up. So all the spent flower-ing shoots are cut back to a strong leading shoot and all other side-shoots are pruned back to two or three buds. In both cases the retained shoots are tied in without delay.

Propagating roses, which is usually done by budding, is perhaps best left to the experts. There are, nevertheless, a few roses, such as the very vigorous earlier floribundas, ramblers, species roses, and miniatures, which will grow from cuttings, but not present-day hybrid teas and floribundas. Grown from cuttings, they are normally not very vigorous, or long-living.

An urgent case for treatment: this rose stem is severely affected by mildew.

Chapter 12
Rock gardens

Sometimes I think we gardeners need our heads examining. We go to enormous lengths to make our hobby more complicated and laborious than it need be.

For instance, we move into a new house with a patch of ground that looks more like a rubbish tip than a garden. The builders have left piles of rubble, bricks and stones, and mounds of earth.

So what do we do? We expend blood, toil, tears and sweat – plus, probably, more money than we can afford – carting away the stones, levelling the earth and creating a nice neat rectangle on which we can develop the garden of our dreams.

At this point we spend pleasant hours poring over books and magazines, searching for ideas. 'Build your own rock garden', we read. What a splendid notion!

So we spend more time, money and physical energy on bringing in some rubble ('a base of good drainage material is essential,' says the book), building a mound of earth, and making several visits to the local builders' merchant to buy local stone ('to blend with the surroundings').

Crazy, isn't it?

I'm not suggesting, of course, that a messy building plot will turn itself into a pretty rock garden without any effort. Nature does need a nudge from us and I for one could do with some tips.

Visiting Harlow Car Gardens, home of the Northern Horticultural Society outside Harrogate (which I commend to you if you're passing that way), I learned a lot from the way they've designed their sandstone and limestone rock gardens.

The sandstone one contains hundreds of plants of every hue. The contours are fundamentally what nature provided, though man has increased fertility and beauty, particularly on the screes which sweep down towards a bridge crossing a little stream.

The guide tells me that at the greatest depth is a layer of broken stone covered with a layer of humus; and on top of this is about a foot of mixed gravel and leaf mould, on top of which is an inch of pure gravel. The scree is used for plants which require sharp drainage and stony soil.

The limestone rock garden at Harlow Car was built to give guidance to those who garden on soil with a high lime content.

Mind you, my garden doesn't stretch over 60 acres like theirs and I haven't a team of nine full-time gardeners to do the work for me, so perhaps I should curb my ambition.

PETER PESKETT:
'A simple, if energetic job'

Interesting thoughts, Michael. And to some extent I agree with your point about clearing builder's rubble from the garden and then bringing it back to build a rockery. So many rock gardens I've seen have, indeed, looked like messy heaps of rubble poorly disguised by the addition of plants. The secret is, of course, to blend the rock into the landscape so that the garden looks as though it has been built around natural outcrops.

There are several different types of stone suitable for rockeries, most of them peculiar to particular localities. Each type has its good and bad points, but there are four I can thoroughly recommend. Westmorland stone, with its grey colour and a surface worn by water to give a super, pitted effect, is probably the most attractive of rockery stones. Welsh limestone is virtually the same as Westmorland, but without the weathered faces. Sandstone, generally red-brown in colour, is a soft, fairly smooth stone and can be obtained in many parts of the country. Derby spar is whitish-grey and has crystalline chips which sparkle in sunlight.

However, the biggest expense in buying rocks is the transport, so it's probably wise to plump for a local stone, which will invariably be cheaper. Also, of course, there is a better chance of it blending into the existing surroundings. Rock can be bought from stone merchants and the bigger garden centres, but remember when ordering to ask for pieces small enough to handle. Most people can manage to place 75-100 lb pieces quite easily.

Sites for rock gardens must be well drained and in a sunny position not overshadowed by trees, fences or walls. And a rockery looks at its best when built on a slope (south-facing is ideal) because then there is more chance of creating the natural outcrop effect.

How big should the site be? Well, this very much depends on personal taste, the size of the garden as a whole, and how much money you are prepared to spend on rocks. Most people have neither the money nor the inclination to turn the whole of their available area into a rock garden, and they happily settle for a comparatively small rockery to provide a break in the monotonous contour of an otherwise flat area.

Building a rockery is a simple, if energetic job. If you have to create a slope, allow the soil several months to settle before starting the actual construction work. When the site is ready, a base – roughly built to the desired contours – should be made of small, coarse stones or other material to provide good drainage.

Starting from the base of the slope, the rocks should then be set in position, each tilted slightly inwards so that rain is diverted to the inside of the rockery. There is no hard

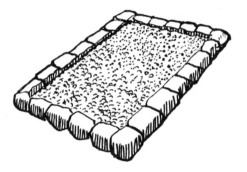

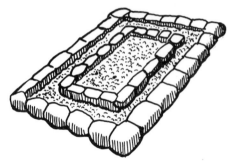

and fast rule about how much of each rock should be buried, but to obtain the outcrop effect you usually have to bury about two-thirds of a large, squarish rock. When placing the rocks, leave enough space between them to support wide, flat pockets of soil for planting– *never* make a mound of soil and stick the rocks in afterwards.

Soil placed in these pockets should be well

If you haven't the space for a large rockery, try building a small raised rock garden. Set out stones in the shape of the bed and fill with soil to the height of the stones. Place a second row of stones 6 inches in from the first row. Position the top stones, half burying them so they appear to be thrusting out of the soil. The last drawing shows what the garden should look like when planted.

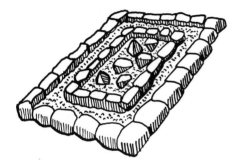 

mixed with peat, and a little bonemeal added. Planting from pots can be done at any time of the year except in freezing weather, though spring is by far the best period. As for the plants themselves, there is a wide range of alpines and other subjects ideal for rock gardens and I've listed a few of my favourites below.

Aetthionema produces pink flowers in May and June.

Alyssum saxatile, lemon yellow or gold, flowers in May.

Anthyllis montana rubra provides clusters

The stone used here is weathered Westmorland limestone. Note how the rocks have been placed sloping slightly backwards to give a natural outcrop effect.

of deep-red flowers in June.

Arabis gives cushions of white flowers.

Arenaria produces mats of foliage with tiny star flowers.

Aster provides splashes of late colour.

Aubretia has cushions in purple-pink-rose shades.

Azalea is a colourful dwarf shrub.

Campanula flowers in summer in blue, mauve and white.

Dianthus (pink) is easy to raise from seed.

Erica (heather) is a 'must' for any rock garden.

Gentiana acaulis gives blue flowers from March to May.

Geranium subcaulescens produces brilliant crimson flowers from July onwards.

Helianthemum is a 'sun rose'.

Helxine solierolii, a vivid green carpeter, is worth growing for its foliage.

Iberis sempervirens is evergreen candytuft

Cut back spring-flowering subjects to near the root when they fade.

The method of constructing a rockery on sloping ground.

with masses of white flowers.

Omphalodes produces blue flowers in spring.

Oxalis floribunda rosea gives rose pink flowers in summer.

Phlox makes a spectacular show in various colours.

Plumbago larpentae gives showy dark blue flowers in autumn.

Primulas are another 'must' for the rockery.

Roses in miniature form are ideal for a prominent position in full sun.

Saponaria ocymoides produces pink or red flowers in May and June.

Saxifraga has many species in different colours.

Sedum is a useful carpeter.

Silene acaulis gives mats of growth with bright pink flowers.

Thymus, a fragrant carpeter, has flowers from white to rose and purple.

Veronica rupestris produces rich blue flowers in June and July.

Violas are also useful for all rock gardens.

By carefully selecting plants from this list, it is possible to create a rockery which will be colourful and full of interest throughout the year. Of course, many gardeners use their rockeries to grow rare or difficult alpines, but this can be an expensive hobby and is not recommended for beginners.

Dealing finally with the care of rock-garden plants, the spring-flowering subjects can be cut back to near the root when they fade, and then new growth will appear. When plants of smother growth, such as aubretia, are cut back, weeds should be cleared away and a little fresh soil used as a top dressing because rockery pockets tend to lose some soil through seepage during heavy rains. Then, in late summer and autumn, when many of the pockets may be comparatively bare, small bulbs can be planted to provide splashes of colour in spring.

slope backwards

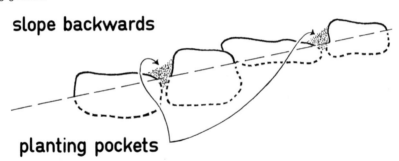

planting pockets

Chapter 13
Greenhouses & frames

At our last house, we had a greenhouse with more mod cons than the home itself. It was the span roof type with electric tubular heating thermostatically controlled, automatic ventilation, soil-warming cables, a capillary watering system, internal rollshades, guttering to collect soft rainwater and goodness knows what else.

Now we've moved to a new home with no greenhouse at all, so I'm shopping around – and getting increasingly confused.

I suppose I could buy the same kind that I had before, but even such an extravagant amenity as that had its drawbacks. For one thing, it had a wooden frame which needed more attention than I had the time to give it.

Aluminium or galvanised steel frames, I'm assured by some of the glossy brochures now piled high on my desk, are far superior. They're lighter. They don't warp or rot. They never need painting. And they're impervious to insects or fungi.

Fine, fine. But there's one other thing about steel houses that the brochures forget to mention: they're considerably more expensive.

Then again, my previous greenhouse had solid walls up to a height of 3 feet or so – cheaper to heat in winter and easier to keep cool in summer, but restricting the variety of plants I could grow in it. Solid walls or glass to the ground? I feel like solving that problem by tossing a coin.

Leafing through some more brochures, though, there seem to be considerable attractions in the lean-to types. They're considerably cheaper, which is always a bonus point for a Yorkshireman, and they should be much easier to heat. On the other hand, wouldn't my plants suffer from curvature of the spine as they reached for the sunlight, always coming from the same direction?

How about a Dutch light house, then? No problem there about the sun pouring in from all angles and it would allow me to grow chrysanthemums and suchlike in the ground. The same seems to apply to those dome-shaped houses which look as though they may have landed in the garden from Outer Space.

Among the accessories I'm encouraged to buy is a translucent polythene liner which 'reduces heat loss and gives consequent economies in heating. A considerable temperature increase can be expected in cold and windy weather.' I'm impressed – but also a little perplexed, because I'd have thought that polythene would have distinct disadvantages by reducing the intensity and quality of the sunlight. Or is that just an old wives' tale?

The type of heating I want is probably the most difficult problem of all. It's so expensive nowadays that I'm tempted to do without it altogether, although I know that will seriously cut down the uses to which I can put my already costly greenhouse.

A paraffin heater would presumably be cheapest, but I don't fancy the smell it makes and I reckon my plants wouldn't either. Electricity cost me a fortune in my last house; oil would almost certainly be even more expensive today, though I might gamble on its becoming cheaper in a year or two's time when the North Sea really starts to pour forth its black gold. (Well, there's no harm in dreaming!)

Whatever type of house I eventually choose, there are still more questions I need answering – like how, and how often, to sterilise the soil; whether I should use soil from the garden; how to prevent my plants becoming scorched in long periods of hot sun, and so on.

Then there's the question of cold frames and cloches. What do they do and how? Maybe I should be in the glass-making business!

GEOFF AMOS:
'Success will come with the personal touch'

A greenhouse (and its most necessary partner, a cold frame) adds the final touch to a garden. It enables the gardener to laugh at the weather, gives all-the-year-round pleasure, and opens up the much more interesting realms of gardening that exist beyond simply digging and planting. The new owner will make mistakes and have his disappointments, but if he persists and perseveres there is no doubt that a greenhouse will bring him a lot of pleasure – and possibly profit!

Nine out of ten greenhouses are bought with the main idea of making them work, at least in part, to help the outdoor garden . . . to start seeds in, to root cuttings, or to keep through the winter plants that will eventually grow outside. Once this main purpose is fulfilled, they are next planted with tomatoes,

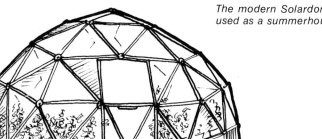

cucumbers perhaps, and pot plants for home decoration. Then, for the autumn and winter, chrysanthemums are moved in from outside.

This kind of growing cycle works very well. With a little easily learned know-how, all these crops fit in with one another, or can be moved to make way for each other. But don't for goodness sake think that it all happens without any cost at all – or without any work. There is heating to pay for (although for the plants I have mentioned it is only necessary for 16-20 weeks out of the 52, possibly less) and there is regular attention to be given.

There are gadgets that will help, at a price, but in the main success will come from the personal touch . . . the regular once or twice-a-day visits.

Although there are many makes of greenhouse they all boil down to only a few types. The double span is the most common, with its sloping roof, straight sides that can be either glass-to-ground or glass down to a 2-3-foot high base of brick, wood or asbestos. You can even have the best of both worlds – glass-to-ground on one side, half glass on the other.

The lean-to greenhouse is perfect for anyone with a wall facing south. It is economical to build and to heat, can be attached to the house and entered through french windows, and again can be glass-to-ground or only part glass.

If I had a good south-facing wall, I would look no further than a lean-to. Light from the south is adequate, the back wall holds heat (reflecting it and keeping the inside air warm), and the artificial heat needed can be run from the normal house supply.

Sometimes the extra warmth can be an embarrassment, and some form of shading is nearly always necessary. But the money saved with a lean-to can be used to provide some form of permanent roll-down shading.

The appearance of a greenhouse is something which not enough people take into account. They worry about the shape, the design, the materials – some of us have even been known to worry about the cost! But looks must come into it too. After all, in most cases, the greenhouse will be in full view in the garden – and I'm not too keen on being able to see all the 'works' through the walls.

Under the staging is a very handy place (sometimes the only place) to store spare pots and boxes, bags of compost and the like, and however tidy you try to keep them they never look very elegant. For my money, therefore, the 3-ft solid wall is something to be desired, if only for the sake of appearance.

There is also undoubtedly a greater heat loss from an all-glass wall, especially in exposed windy places and, although I must admit that the extra light is good for plants growing on the floor (particularly lettuce, and possibly also tomatoes when they are first planted), on balance I can do without it.

And glass-to-ground is a dead loss for anyone growing only pot plants. They must be up on staging where they can be examined, watered and attended to properly, and light is of no value at all underneath them. The compromise now obtainable of all glass one side and a wall the other will possibly suit a lot of growers.

The choice of materials provides another headache for the new buyer, and again I am influenced by their looks.

Plastic houses, as they are at the moment, are hardly a runner in this race. Their one asset is that they are cheap, but unhappily they look cheap too. Plants will certainly grow in them, and the claimed loss of light doesn't stand up in my view. But plastic houses are liable to gale damage, they lose and gain heat quicker than is good for some plants and

Traditional span greenhouse, with glass to ground.

there is a problem of condensation. If you want an inexpensive greenhouse in a hurry, well yes, a 'plastic' will do. But if the greenhouse bug bites, and it generally does, you'll soon want a better one.

Polythene houses have, of course, been a life-saver for the commercial grower. A large area can be covered quickly, easily and inexpensively and they are ideal for the salad and vegetable crops commercially grown inside.

Concrete houses are other non-starters in the good-looker's race. They are, of course, stronger and less destructible than anything else and need absolutely no maintenance. But the concrete is bulkier than, ideally, it should be, although the latest models are gradually becoming more elegant.

Metal houses with the 'no maintenance' tag have stormed the amateur gardening world in recent years. Most are made of aluminium but there are some built in steel and in aluminium and steel alloy. They are more expensive, size for size, than other materials, but because there are no maintenance costs they work out cheaper in the end.

Their appearance does, however, deteriorate over the years as the metal is affected by oxidisation, although this is now being overcome on some of them by a method of plating with a bonded paint covering. Glass repairs

and erection are easy, and the light ratio is first class because the glazing bars are narrow. But heat loss is high, particularly in glass-to-ground houses, condensation is fairly high (only in the more expensive types is provision made for this), and holes have to be drilled in strategic places for the fixing of wires and shelves.

For me the good quality wooden white-lead-painted greenhouses (the old-fashioned type if you like) are the best of all. If your budget will stand it, choose one built from the very best wood although, if well-made, ordinary deal and pine can be excellent.

A well-kept greenhouse of this type is an asset to any garden. The appearance of clean glass set off by sparkling white paint takes a lot of beating. Although I've cursed the two-yearly painting chore as much as anyone, if good white-lead paint is used inside and out a wooden house will last almost for ever.

Wooden houses are warmer than other types and are supremely adaptable inside. Shelves, struts, wires, temporary shading and polythene lining are easily fixed if thought necessary, but I don't need this to 'sell' them to me . . . they *look* right, and that's almost enough.

If you like the look of them, red cedar greenhouses (the non-paintable type) have all the advantages of a wooden type without the chore of regular painting, although they need coating with linseed oil or treatment with a proprietary preservative now and again.

The size of the greenhouse you buy is purely a matter of individual choice. The most common remark I hear is the wish that a bigger one had been chosen, and certainly as the interest grows so does the need for more space.

The lean-to, perfect for anyone with a south-facing wall.

The smallest houses sold measure around 6 ft by 6 ft and are, as a rule, almost too compact to be practicable. The business of even wielding a watering can becomes hazardous, and backing out of the door is a necessity. Really, 8 ft by 6 ft is the minimum sensible size, and 10 ft by 8 ft is better. But for me 12 ft by 8 ft is approaching the ideal for the average amateur grower.

Watch the height, too. Nothing is worse than trying to work inside a greenhouse that is too small for you to stand up in, and if you fancy your chances with chrysanthemums remember that some of them grow to 6 or 7 ft quite easily. Size is, of course, controlled by the price you want to pay, but it's well worth remembering that doubling the size doesn't double the price.

The traditional cloche with glass and wire (left), and the new one-piece plastic model (right).

Something that does mount up is the extras. Staging, shelves, guttering, down pipes and water tanks are seldom included in the advertised price. You cannot do without them, although the handy chap can knock up staging easily enough.

The other extra – and the biggest of all – is the heating apparatus. It has to be bought, maintained and kept supplied with fuel – an ever-rising cost these days. The question may well be asked whether it is worth providing any heat at all. Can enough be done with a cold house alone to make it worth having?

The answer is all around, almost everywhere you look. The smallest and most modest of structures is generally warmed up for a few weeks, in March and early April, and this alone alters anyone's whole gardening outlook. Those few weeks of heat mean that you can raise plants from seeds and cuttings that you would otherwise have to buy. They allow you to pick and choose your favourite varieties to raise, instead of having to put up with what someone else has chosen to grow. And

they give you that valuable gain of a few weeks with crops that you look forward to having a bit earlier than our outside climate will allow. Yes, some form of heating is certainly worthwhile.

The least expensive to install is the paraffin lamp. A Blue Flame type with a 2-inch diameter wick will keep an 8 ft by 8 ft house warm enough to grow everything the average gardener wants. It must be kept clean and topped up with fuel, and it is always as well to sacrifice a fraction of the warmth by leaving a top ventilator open to take away any fumes. Make no mistake, properly managed, a paraffin heater can be used to grow anything. I know a top grower of orchids who uses nothing else.

As one who spent years and years of his youth being responsible for the great coke boilers that kept a range of greenhouses warm, and in which grew almost everything possible out of season, as well as grapes, peaches, oranges, pineapples and orchids, and who still remembers the agonies of waking up on freezing cold mornings hoping against hope that the fires had performed properly, I can only say that I have had my fill of them! But what I will say is this: in no other greenhouse I have been in since has that lovely 'growing' atmosphere been so apparent. Plants of all sorts seem to love the warmth from hot water pipes.

It is well worth considering gas which, since it has begun to come from the North Sea, can be burned inside the greenhouse in convenient little heaters whose flame goes up and down automatically to keep the temperature steady, and which cut off the gas supply in the unlikely event of the flame going out. And far from harming plants, as we've always been told gas does, the North Sea variety is now advertised as helping them to grow by adding carbon dioxide to their diet.

Possibly – and this is the ultimate, of course – greenhouses may be fitted up in the modern manner with thermostatically controlled electrical tube heaters boosted automatically (and hang the expense!) by a fan heater that comes on when needed and which, incidentally, can blow cool air around in the summer.

It all depends on what you are willing to pay, both for the original equipment and also to keep it running. If you want it the easy way you have to pay for it; but if you shoulder some of the work and responsibility yourself it is cheaper. The golden rule is that the factor which controls what you can grow is the temperature to which your house falls on the coldest night of the year. Think about it . . .

If you find room for a greenhouse, then you must also find room somewhere for a cold frame. Plants that are raised in a warm house can't suddenly be stood or planted outside, however kind the weather. They need a halfway house to soften the blow. And as the job of most greenhouses is, at least in part, to raise plants that are eventually going to have to brave the weather (early vegetable plants, bedding plants, chrysanthemums, dahlias and the like) the cold frame is a must.

Now this is something on which you *can* save money. I know I insisted earlier that the looks of garden structures were important, and certainly neat and tidy brick-built cold frames covered with white-painted glass lights can add to the pleasing picture. But cold frames don't *have* to be permanent. You only need them around from about the beginning of April to the middle of May, the six weeks or so immediately before you plant things out. And four 18-inch wide wooden sides covered with a sheet of polythene will do this hardening off job quite well. Then they can be packed up and put away until next year.

Of course, if they are permanent you can grow cucumbers or melons in them through the summer, and/or keep your cyclamen and cinerarias, primulas, calceolarias and solanums cool and shaded until they go into the warmth in late September. So perhaps a compromise is the answer, with one or two good permanent frames and the rest temporary, knocked-up affairs that can be packed up when finished with.

Cloches do much the same job as frames, but are not quite such a biting necessity (more of a luxury in fact), and yet almost indispensable if you are committed to growing early vegetables. However, setting them up, taking them down again, setting seeds or plants at unheard of and awkward spacings to make the best use of their size, moving them to weed and water, to say nothing of finding somewhere to store them, can give you quite a bit of trouble, but they *can* gain you a week or two with such things as early salads, carrots, cauliflowers, peas and beans. They can cover strawberries in February to ripen them a week earlier, or they'll preserve your row of parsley through the winter.

When they were jigsaw puzzles of bent bits of wire and dangerous sheets of glass, I hated the sight of them. The latest one-piece plastics have altered the whole picture – in fact, I'm saving up for one!

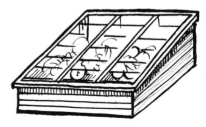

A cold frame is essential if you've got a greenhouse.

Chapter 14
Pests & diseases

Waiter, there's a fly in my soup – not to mention caterpillars in my cabbages, botrytis on my strawberries, mealy bugs on my cacti and capsid on my currants.

Birds are pecking the young fruit from my gooseberries, moles are making an unholy mess of my lawn, and ants are tunnelling fatally under my herbaceous border. What am I to do?

I've already found, through letters reacting to my *Garden News* column, that expert advice on how to destroy wasps' nests, whitefly infestations and the like is avidly read, but tips on how to eliminate slightly larger creatures (especially birds) bring a storm of protests, with the protectionists in full cry.

My friend Will Tagg, who is pest officer for the new town of Bracknell and the surrounding Berkshire countryside, is a passionate animal lover who has spent much of his life ridding gardens and farmsteads of undesirable wild life without ever being accused of cruelty.

Sometimes, I suspect, he's had a bit of luck on his side. There was the case, for instance, of the old lady who sought his advice on how to save her lawn from ruination by moles without harming the poor creatures.

'Borrow a mower with a heavy roller,' said Will. 'It will give the moles a headache and they'll go away.'

And, would you believe it, they did! The old lady was delighted. 'They're burrowing away happily in my neighbour's garden now,' she reported with glee. What her neighbour said is not recorded . . .

In our part of the world, foxes are a growing menace, even in town gardens, now that motorway construction has driven them out of many a covert and at the same time seriously restricted the activities of the Hunt. Now that's a subject guaranteed to arouse popular passion!

Will is unashamedly a hunting man. 'One bite on a fox's neck from a good hound', he says, 'will kill it instantaneously. If I'm called out to deal with foxes on private premises, the first thing I do is contact the local Hunt. If they won't tackle the job, I have to do something myself – but I can tell you, it takes a good man to gas a litter of cubs. It breaks my heart.'

Because of the mild winters, Will's been working overtime in recent years destroying wasps' nests. But in this work he now has a powerful ally – the badger, now happily protected.

'I know Brock takes the odd chicken now and again, but he kills rats and mice at the same time – and he's the finest thing out for taking a wasps' nest.'

I suppose we all sleep fairly soundly in our beds, untroubled by guilty thoughts, if pests in the garden are destroyed by other creatures. That's nature getting the balance right.

But from a gardener's point of view, nature doesn't always co-operate. Lately, indeed, she's been positively obstructive and most of my vegetables will disappear if I don't do something to rid them of the pests that plague us.

I know there are countless chemicals on the market which, if we're to believe the advertisements, should rid us of pests and diseases at the touch of a pressurised dispenser. But they don't. Not for me they don't, anyway.

Is it because I'm using the wrong pesticides? Am I applying them at the wrong times and in the wrong quantities? Or could it be, as I suspect, that many pests and diseases are becoming immune to them?

Above all, there must be some basic rules of hygiene in the garden which would prevent many of our horticultural ills, and I'd like to know what they are.

JEAN STOWE:
'Prevention is better than cure'

Well Michael, you have hit a barrage of balls into my court, and I shall pick up the last one first. That is, basic rules of hygiene. Because, if you observe these, ravage by pest and disease can be greatly reduced. Prevention is always better than cure, and these eight basic rules should help you.

Rule 1 – Weed control: weeds shelter pests and harbour diseases. It is no good resting ground from brassicas, in an effort to starve out club root, if the disease is being perpetuated by cruciferous weeds such as shepherd's purse. Another example is bryony, invariably infected with cucumber mosaic virus. This is spread by aphids to a wide range of cultivated plants, resulting in the death of susceptible subjects such as cucumbers and marrows.

Rule 2 – Tidiness: piles of rubble, plant debris, leaves, etc, are another breeding ground of pests and diseases. Prune out and burn dead wood from trees and shrubs, treating wounds with a pruning paint. Dig up and burn any dead plant – it may have a root disease. Old tree stumps can harbour honey fungus, a parasite which attacks the roots and kills woody plants. Annuals and vegetables should be lifted, roots and all, at the end of the season. Burn anything you suspect of carrying pest or disease and put the rest on the compost heap.

Rule 3 – Strong, healthy plants are less likely to succumb to pest or disease than weak ones: so attend to feeding, mulching and watering.

Rule 4 – Plant good quality stock in the first place.

Rule 5 – Prepare the ground well and plant carefully.

Rule 6 – Rotation is as important in the flower garden as it is in the vegetable plot for it provides less opportunity for pests and diseases to build up.

Rule 7 – Seed dressings: these give a good start, particularly with peas and beans.

Rule 8 – A stitch in time saves nine: spray early before pests and diseases become

The plant on the right is suffering from club-root. On the left is the root system of a healthy plant. (Photo courtesy of ICI.)

entrenched. It may even be possible to cut off and burn affected growths, thus avoiding or delaying the need to spray.

The question of chemical remedies can confuse you as there are so many to choose from. It is essential to obtain the right one for the job. Are you dealing with a pest, to be killed with a pesticide, or is it a fungus disease requiring a fungicide? Viruses cannot be eliminated by chemical sprays and, usually, affected plants must be destroyed. Physiological disorders are connected with water and food supplies, soil conditions and the weather, and these can only be put right by cultural treatments.

For simple disorders, booklets with good photographs are produced by several of the chemical manufacturers. Unfortunately, there is nothing similar for diseases. For technical details Ministry of Agriculture Advisory Leaflets can be helpful, obtainable free from the Ministry of Agriculture, Tolcarne Drive, Pinner, Middx, HA5 2DT.

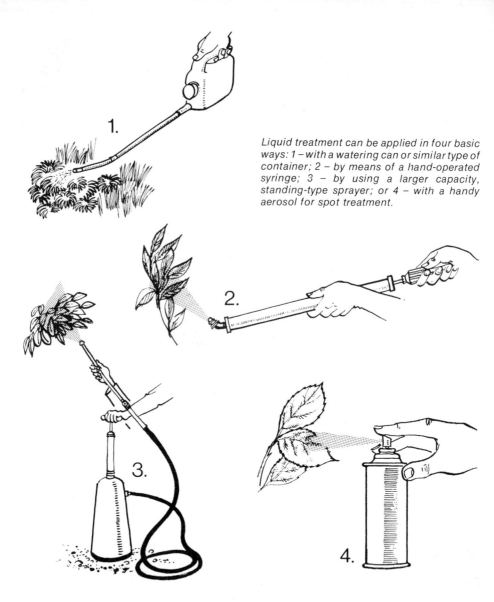

Liquid treatment can be applied in four basic ways: 1 – with a watering can or similar type of container; 2 – by means of a hand-operated syringe; 3 – by using a larger capacity, standing-type sprayer; or 4 – with a handy aerosol for spot treatment.

Diagnosis is not always easy and, if in doubt, seek professional advice. There is no National Health Service for garden plants, but the Royal Horticultural Society gives free advice on garden problems. Specimens should be sent, in a dry polythene bag, to the Director, RHS Garden, Wisley, Ripley, Woking, Surrey. And *Garden News* operates a useful reader advice bureau.

But, even armed with details of the pest or disease and the recommended control, you still have to select a suitable product. Rarely is the shop assistant knowledgeable. Indeed, can we reasonably expect him to be? The matter is confused by the practice of selling under proprietary or brand names. However, the manufacturers do state the active ingredients somewhere on the label, so study the small print. Another point is that many products contain more than one chemical, eg, a systemic insecticide controlling aphids may contain BHC to kill caterpillars as well. Again

If you have geraniums with leaf damage like this, then the culprit is likely to be the common green capsid.

it is worth taking time in choosing the product
– you may find that you can kill two or more
pests with one treatment.

Having obtained the correct chemical, will
it work? *The chemical must be used as
directed!* Read the instructions as if they were
a legal document, noting any limitations or
precautions. Do not spray in hot sunshine or
when plants are dry at the roots.

There are many examples of insects
developing resistance to chemicals, and
recently fungi have shown signs of resisting
systemic fungicides. But this is more likely to
occur on the farm, where the same chemical
is continually applied, than in the garden.
Nevertheless, it is worth changing insecticides from time to time, particularly in
greenhouses.

It is impossible to discuss all the chemicals
available to gardeners. In any case new ones
are continually coming on to the market. But
it might help to outline the good standbys
likely to be found in a keen gardener's
medicine chest.

Sucking insects such as aphids, whitefly,
red spider mite, scale insects, etc, are controlled most efficiently by systemic insecticides.
These chemicals are absorbed into the sap of
the plant, and taken up by the insect when
feeding. Malathion, although not systemic, is
very useful, and also kills caterpillars.

*A regular pest is the Common White cabbage
butterfly. It lays its eggs on the leaves which
are then rapidly eaten away by the emerging
caterpillars. Treat at the first signs.*

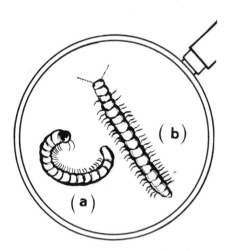

*Millipedes attack plants underground, caus-
ing considerable damage to tubers, bulbs and
large seeds. Millipedes (a) are slightly smaller
and paler than centipedes (b).*

DDT was withdrawn from the garden market in 1971 because of its persistence in the environment. The related, but less persistent BHC (lindane) is still available against a wide range of sucking and biting insects, also soil pests. Alternatives to DDT include trichlorphon (dipterex), sevin (carbaryl) dust, and fenitrothion (fentro) for the control of caterpillars, earwigs, woodlice, capsids, etc. Of particular interest is bromophos, for soil pests, with no risk of taint. Remember that root crops cannot be grown on land treated with BHC for at least 18 months.

On the fungicide front there is captan for rose black spot and karathane for powdery mildews. Zineb, maneb or thiram may be necessary for potato blight, downy mildews, leaf spots and rusts. Systemic fungicides have appeared on the scene later than systemic insecticides, and show promise for the control of many diseases, including powdery mildews, tomato leafmould, Botrytis diseases, wilt of carnations and some bulb diseases. Benomyl (benlate) is probably the best known.

Odds and bobs you might need include cheshunt compound for the damping-off of seedlings, formalin for soil sterilisation, slug bait and pruning paint. Two tips: a dash of washing-up liquid makes sprays cover the plant evenly, particularly when applying fungicides; and aerosols, although expensive, save the tedious measuring and mixing of sprays. I usually treat myself to one at the beginning of the season, for spot treatment of aphids. This way, numbers never build up – in theory, anway! Aerosols are practical in greenhouses, and so are smokes. TCNB (tecnazene) checks grey mould (Botrytis) and azobenzene the red spider mite.

Ardent environmentalists, of whom I am one, should be reassured that every effort is being made to discover safer, less persistent pesticides. The question of the 'balance of nature' should be regarded in its proper context. By gardening in any form, we seek to alter and harness nature to our own ends. Perhaps I should refer to developments in biological control. Parasites of the glasshouse red spider mite and glasshouse whitefly are usually obtainable from the RHS Garden, Wisley, and from Springfield Nursery, Pick Hill, Waltham Abbey, Essex.

As for larger creatures, it really does depend on the circumstances. For the first time in our lives we have a fairly large, wild garden. And for the first time in our lives, we have a mole. To begin with I was all set to trap it. However on reading up the subject – those Ministry leaflets again – I concluded that, as considerable experience and patience is required, I probably wouldn't succeed anyway. On the other hand, if we had a small garden, full of rare plants, then I would be searching for a pest officer!

But, think twice before calling in the Hunt. My husband spent his pre-college practical year on a large market garden and he recalls with glee the occasion the local Hunt came careering across the fields, completely out of control. Leeks were flying in all directions!

Rabbits and deer are a nuisance in some areas. A sure, but expensive answer is to erect good fencing. Many devices have been tried against birds, but again the physical barrier of a fruit cage is impossible to beat. Or you can throw wire or plastic netting over vulnerable crops such as lettuce and cabbages.

Two hazards Michael doesn't mention are pets and children. Most of us know that bitches leave brown patches on lawns, but are you aware that cat urine blackens evergreens and conifers? I had the base of a beautiful Ceanothus impressus ruined by our neighbours' prize Siamese. I wouldn't have believed it if I hadn't caught him in the act! And have you ever heard of dogs eating aubretia? Well, mine do!

Children perhaps should be regarded as synonymous with footballs. A friend of ours with five children just gave up – grassed down the vegetable garden and took an allotment. But seriously, careful planning can avoid unnecessary damage. Children don't keep to paths, so I always place stepping stones at strategic points in the flower borders. Also I allow space for sand pits, swings and the paraphernalia that goes with 'play'.

Chapter 15
Flower arranging

My friend Percy Thrower once wrote – and I pulled his leg about it – that 'gardening is now rated as, if not No 1, certainly No 2 hobby throughout the British Isles'. I thought I knew what No 1 must be, but it seems I was wrong.

Consider this extraordinary statement made by Mr Mark J. Weston in a booklet called *Summer Flower Arranging Step by Step:*

'Flower arranging is justifiably rated as the most popular leisure time activity among discriminating people.' Well, well! Clearly I must find out more about this 'pastime that brings peace of mind from the hurly burly of the daily routine'.

I have another good reason for wanting to learn more of the skills of this gentle art: my No 2 son has been learning pottery at A level at school and has produced a succession of big vases, little vases, fat vases, thin vases, bulbous ones and rectangular ones, vases in fact of every shape and size. I'm sure they'd look better with flowers in them.

But what kind of flowers? How am I to arrange them so that they don't look as though I just stuffed them into the container as a temporary measure and then forgot about them?

How am I to ensure a longer life for the flowers? How often am I supposed to change the water, if I'm to use water at all?

What I usually do with cut flowers before putting them in water is to make an incision at the base of the stem. I'm not quite sure why I do this, except that it's what Grandma used to do.

When we visit village halls for *Gardeners' Question Time,* the stage is usually decorated by the flower arrangement section of the horticultural society who are our hosts, and I study the shapes they create with great care. Then I go home and try to emulate them with marked lack of success. I really must be taken back to first principles.

I also suspect there's an element of cheating among the discriminating people who pursue this hobby. I hear whispers of plastic foam being used to hold the flowers in position, of pinholders, special scissors and even chicken wire.

Could this be true? And what substance is there in the ugly rumour I've heard that flower arrangers actually use paint to add colour to foliage?

After all has been revealed and the expert advice provided, I'm going to try again – though I have a feeling that the arrangement I produce will be technically known as 'asymmetrical'.

JULIA CLEMENTS:
'An opening for creativity'

I am glad to learn that Michael Barratt is interested in flower arranging, for this is the end product of flower gardening and everyone likes making their home more beautiful by bringing the garden indoors.

If Michael doesn't know what makes the subject so popular, I'll tell him. It's because everyone can do it. Whether you have a big or a small garden, or none at all, you can find the basic materials with which to make a living picture with flowers.

All of us have a certain amount of creative ability but mostly we cannot dash out and buy paints and canvases, nor can we take up learning the piano and find immediate expression. But we can pick or buy a few flowers, make a creative arrangement with them, and get a result almost at once. It is the easy availability of the basic materials which gives flower arranging its appeal.

If, when feeling a bit low, a housewife goes out and buys, say, five irises, and cuts the stems to different lengths, placing them on a pin holder standing in the base of a shallow dish, then adds some stones or a piece of wood low down to unite the stems, she is creating a design. Had she just stuffed them into a container, as Michael says, she would have gained no satisfaction at all. So, one of

the first answers to the popularity of flower arranging is that it is an expressive art.

Later she will add some bulrushes to the irises, or some twisted dried vine tendrils. She might place a china frog or bird low in the dish or even in the water to make a 'scene'. Once her eyes are opened to the tremendous possibilities of the subject, there is no end to the interest. She – or he, don't forget – may then be led to an interest in containers, and many take up the study of pottery as an extra hobby. She will learn about colour and its effects on our sensibilities. Different designs and shapes with flowers are studied, not just for the exercise but because varying shapes are needed if they are to take their proper place in the home, ie, horizontal for the table, vertical for a narrow corner, triangular for the centre of a side table against a wall, asymmetrical triangle for one end of a table or a shelf, and so on.

Michael asks what kind of flowers should he use? There are many hundreds of different varieties, and it all depends which are available at the time. I might write and say use some Berberis paniculata at the sides, and you might reply, 'What is that?'. It was this which led me early in my career to suggest that people open their eyes to different forms, shapes and sizes. Never mind about the exact names if you are just beginning – this will all come later – but do look for some tall flowers or twigs for the outline, some bigger or more important flowers for the centre, and some smaller or less important varieties for filling

If you have only one kind of flower and the stems are all the same length, then the trick is in the cutting. Cut the stems so that some are tall, some medium and some short. You cannot create an attractive arrangement with everything the same height; even if you are painting there must be different levels, and varying dimensions. So it is with flower arranging: leaves create depth and grasses or light thin flowers give highlights. All this will help you to appreciate the different forms and shapes which give a three-dimensional

appearance to your flower arrangement. Do you begin to see how absorbing it all is?

The use of plastic foam and pinholders to hold the flowers in place is not cheating; it is common sense. You can't make an omelette without a frying pan, neither can you obtain an artistic flower arrangement without something to hold the flowers firmly in the intended position. Yes, we have come a long way since we stuck flowers in an upright vase and left them until they went sour!

Today, after picking or buying flowers, you should recut the stem ends (preferably under water to avoid an air lock) and leave them in deep water for some hours before arranging them. This allows the stems to become fully charged with water, which helps them to live longer. Add a tablet of charcoal to the water to

Some of the basic items that the newcomer to flower arranging will need.

WIRE STEMS ON PINHOLDER STEM TO HOLD WIRE IN PLACE

PLASTIC FOAM ON TO PINHOLDER

absorb any poisons and bacteria and so keep it pure longer, which in turn extends the fresh life of the flowers.

I cannot go into the intricacies of all the different kinds of flowers, but in general soft-stemmed varieties should be recut and stood in water for some hours before using. Woody-stemmed flowers, branches and twigs should be recut, the stem ends split and again stood in deep water, while most leaves (not the grey woolly type) should be submerged for some hours – or overnight – in deep water, to which a little sugar has been added to stiffen them. The sugar creates a thin film over the pores and avoids loss of moisture through transpiration.

Many other tricks are learned as you go along, such as putting water in the vases before making the arrangement to avoid the stems becoming dry. Add water to the foam daily, otherwise it will sap moisture from the flowers. Pick flowers late at night or early in the morning when transpiration is at its lowest, and do *not* change the water once the arrangement is made; just add tepid water each day.

I would suggest that the beginner does not start with an asymmetrical design, as Michael thinks he might do, for it is one of the most difficult and requires a knowledge of balance and rhythm. Start with the basics of tall, medium, and short flowers and, when these principles are firmly in your mind, you will never again walk in your garden without noticing something that will fall into place in your creative flower arrangement.

Four popular styles of flower arrangement: Tall (top left), Bowl (top right), Fan (bottom left) and Pedestal.

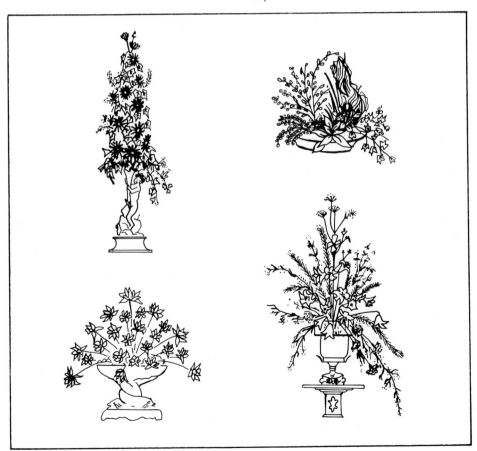

Chapter 16
Design & construction

Once upon a time, in the dear dead days beyond recall, poor people were huddled together in little back-to-back or terrace houses, stretching for row upon row along cobbled streets.

For gardens they had window boxes – and concrete back yards.

Gradually, builders and town planners began to see the light and to appreciate the need for more space in which the workers could enjoy at least a modicum of leisure through gardening.

New planning regulations called for 'frontages' – and a much lower density of housing, with the result that lawns and flower beds or vegetable patches replaced the old back yards.

But there were problems. Land was being used up at an alarming rate. 'Suburban sprawl' became a vile phrase. So the planners went to work again and produced a new life-style for the 'sixties and 'seventies.

They called the new homes 'town houses'. Well, yes, they were huddled together and sometimes even back-to-back, but at least they had a new name. So did the back yards, which were called 'patios'.

And so nowadays we need advice on how to construct paths and patios, walls and fences, to blend with our new environment. (If you had six children, plus dogs and cats, as I have, you'd appreciate that there can be quite a forceful argument for a garden consisting of concrete and green paint!)

There's another good reason for learning more about design and construction in the garden: calling in a builder or landscape gardener to do the job for you can be an alarmingly expensive operation nowadays.

When it comes to laying paths, I fancy the crazy paving variety – because that's what my workmanship would look like in any case, even if I used square concrete slabs. However, I have an uneasy feeling that crazy paving isn't half as easy as it looks.

I mean, it has to have some sort of foundation, hasn't it? What should it consist of? How deep should it be?

One of the problems in the Thames Valley where I live is that the water table is very high – in places just an inch or two – so drainage obviously needs special attention.

Spreading tarmacadam looks relatively easy, but we had a driveway done professionally that way and it began to break up after the first frosts. How's that to be avoided?

I've also had a lot of trouble with my fencing. Mine came in panels of interwoven wood and I did all the right things like creosoting it, but now it's falling down. The wood seems to have shrunk so that the panels no longer meet. Could I have avoided that?

I don't think I'd attempt building a brick wall, but I'd like to know what to do with one once somebody else had built it for me: what's the effect, for instance, of creepers – particularly ivy? I can never make up my mind whether it helps to hold up an old wall, or whether it breaks up the mortar with ultimately dire effects.

I'm quite breathtakingly ignorant, aren't I!

GEOFF HAMILTON:
'Start with a good foundation'

With garden construction the important thing is to think and plan before you start, and to consider how best you can blend your garden layout with the house. If you have a modern residence, why dress it up to look like Wuthering Heights? There is an abundance of modern materials that will match the architecture of your late 20th century house far, far better, and for the do-it-yourselfer they're much easier to use. If you fancy crazy paving, it will look fine if your house is old, and especially if it's rural. If it's new, my advice is to stick to rectangular paving.

Michael's point about foundations is one of the most important, especially if the house is brand new, for the footings will have been dug out by machine and refilled afterwards.

This means that the surrounding soil will in time inevitably settle a few inches, however hard you may try to compact it. Without a good concrete foundation the paving will settle too, although if you have a really hard base you may well get away with less.

Let me begin with some general advice on the necessary preparation for a patio foundation in a new garden, which you can adjust to your specific needs.

The first thing is to mark out the area you want to pave and then fix the correct levels. You can't take too much trouble over this job, as a patio that slopes towards the house and is not far enough below the damp-proof course (DPC) will result in a lake of water outside, and a damp patch inside.

You can easily recognise the DPC on most houses because the layer of mortar between the bricks is noticeably thicker. If the walls have a rough-cast finish, this will usually not continue below DPC level. The recommended finished level of a patio is two courses of bricks below the DPC.

To make sure your levels are right, you must work to pegs. First of all excavate the area to approximately the correct level, which will be about 14 inches below DPC (you'll see why in a minute). Now cut some pegs about 2 feet long, and mark a line 3 inches from the top of each. Set the first peg near the house, so that the top is just two courses below DPC. Using a straight edge and spirit level, you can now put in the rest of the pegs about 5 feet apart each way. Don't forget to slope slightly away from the house (about half a bubble on the spirit level will do).

When all the pegs have been set out, you can start concreting. You will need 4 inches of concrete foundation, so make sure that you have excavated to a depth 4 inches below the line marked on the pegs. Now fill with concrete up to that mark, using a 6:1 mix of ballast and cement and keeping it fairly dry. There is no need to make a good finish on this layer because it will be covered anyway, but do keep it level. Bash the concrete down well

Method of erecting fencing on a slope, each panel dropping a few inches.

slope

gravel board

(I use the back of a rake) and allow it to set overnight.

You are now ready to start laying the paving. Not all houses are built absolutely straight, especially the older ones, so make sure that the paving will be properly aligned. Stretch a line about half-an-inch from the house wall and work to that. It's worth taking a lot of trouble over the lining up and levelling of the first slab. If you're an eighth of an inch out on that one, you will be much further adrift by the time you reach the other end.

Many people will recommend that you lay the slabs on sand. I have found that the easiest and most permanent way is by what is known as the 'five point method'. Prepare some mortar, using a 3:1 mix of soft sand and cement, again keeping it fairly dry. Then place on the ground a blob of mortar about 2 inches high at each corner and another in the middle of where the first slab will sit.

Now comes the difficult part. The slab must be tapped down until it is level with the top of the nearest peg. The ideal tool for this job is a 3-lb club-hammer. Use the handle end, not the head, which would mark or possibly even break the slab.

To check the level, place a straight edge across the slab to the top of the nearest peg. This level must be carefully checked both ways. When the straight edge lies snugly across the slab and you can't see any light beneath it, it's level.

The remainder of the paving can now be laid in the same way, butting each new slab closely against the one you've just laid. As you reach the pegs, either knock them down into the concrete or simply break them off.

There is a wide choice of patterns you can follow when laying the paving. The easiest is to use 2 ft by 2 ft slabs throughout, simply set in 'tramlines'. This does tend to look a bit 'local authority' though, so to avoid the patio resembling a miniature shopping precinct I like to vary the sizes of slabs in a random pattern. You can either work out the pattern first, or simply develop it as you go along. Try to avoid long lines, particularly across the width of the patio. This means that you will have to think a couple of slabs ahead, but you'll soon get the hang of it.

Remember that if you are buying new slabs there is a choice of colour as well as size. Most new slabs are now made to metric measurements, which are not compatible for matching up with, for example, secondhand or existing imperial slabs. Many amateurs make the mistake of buying the biggest possible slabs on the basis of being able to cover the ground quicker. Among the common imperial sizes are 1 ft by 18 inches, 2 ft by 2 ft or 3 ft by 2 ft. Unless you're built like an ox, you'll find it far easier to handle and lay, for example, three lighter 2 ft by 2 ft slabs than two heavy 3 ft by 2 ft ones!

Crazy paving is a different kettle of fish. It does have the one advantage that, if you can pick up broken slabs from your local council yard and lay them yourself, it is quite cheap. I feel that it never looks as attractive as rectangular paving, but it is a matter of opinion.

The foundation should be prepared in the same way as for rectangular paving. But before you start paving sort out the bigger pieces and use them on the outer edges. The technique of levelling is exactly as previously described, but instead of using the 'five point method' spread a layer of mortar under the whole piece. Leave about half-an-inch or so between the pieces as you lay them, to allow for pointing in later.

The thing that is going to drive *you* crazy is fitting the pieces together. Keep a hammer and a brick bolster handy so that you can cut off the odd corner that won't fit, rather than sorting through the whole pile every time to find a suitable piece. Check every piece with the straight edge as you go. It's very easy to go wrong, and bad levels show up like a sore thumb. (And take care, or you may have one of those by the time you've finished!)

When all the paving is down, leave it to set for a couple of days and then you can start pointing. The mix here should be rather stronger than has been used up to now – a 1:1 ratio of soft sand and cement, mixed quite wet. Work it in well with the trowel between the pieces of paving. Before it has fully set it can be 'lined in' by simply marking a line down the centre of the pointing with a piece of thick bent wire. This may sound rather unnecessary, but it makes a world of difference to the finish.

If you plan on having a large expanse of paving, whether rectangular or crazy, it can look a bit hard. I like to soften the appearance by leaving the odd small space, filling it with soil and planting either rock plants or prostrate conifers.

It sounds as if Michael's tarmac was laid by some pretty unprofessional 'professionals'. Again, the secret of success lies in the foundation work. If you are going to run your car on it, you must first put down at least 6 inches of good hardcore, followed by a 1½-inch layer of 'basecoat tarmac' topped by ¾ inch of 'topcoat'.

Set your level pegs as before, but this time

Paving arranged in a pattern looks far better than formal squares laid side by side in rows.

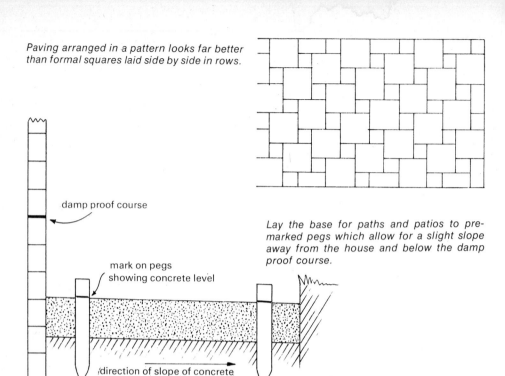

damp proof course

Lay the base for paths and patios to pre-marked pegs which allow for a slight slope away from the house and below the damp proof course.

mark on pegs
showing concrete level

direction of slope of concrete

It is essential that slabs are level when laid on points of cement. The top diagram shows the correct way, with the slabs close to the flat edge. Below it the wrong approach is illustrated, as only one side of the slab is at the correct height.

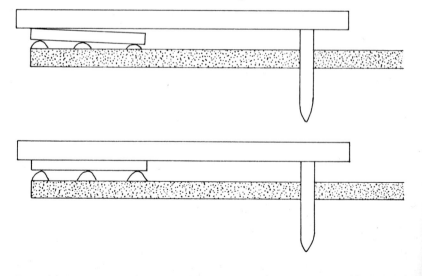

mark them ¾ inch and 2¼ inches from the top. If, as is often the case, you need a slope on the driveway, you won't be able to check the pegs with a spirit level. Instead, set a peg at the finished level at the top and bottom of the slope and stretch a tight line between them. Then set the other pegs to the line.

Make sure you have excavated at least 8½ inches below the top of the pegs, then lay in 6 inches of hardcore. If it is fairly coarse, blind it over with a little ballast or hoggin, and then roll it. The best machine for this job is a pedestrian-controlled vibrating roller which can be hired without much trouble.

Now you are ready to lay the basecoat. This consists of ¾-inch granite chips coated with tar. Simply spread it out with a rake, to a depth of 1½ inches, keeping it as level as possible with the help of the pegs.

You will find that your tools get sticky and difficult to use, so keep a little fire going nearby to melt the 'goo' off your shovel and rake. If you have a fair area to lay it's also a good idea to cover the pile of tarmac with an old tarpaulin or polythene sheet, which will keep it warm and much easier to handle.

Roll the basecoat and spread ¾ inch of ⅜-inch topcoat tarmac in exactly the same way. This should again be rolled and then left for a few days to harden off before you run your car on it.

If you are laying tarmac on an existing concrete base the basecoat can be dispensed with, but the concrete must first be covered with a 'tack' coat. Put this on with an old watering can and a broom, and it will 'stick' the tarmac to the concrete.

If you think you've got trouble with your fencing now, just wait till you come to replace it! Timber prices have rocketed up and the cost of labour has risen too, so fencing is almost a rich man's luxury now. The good old feather-edge-on-arris-rail type has virtually priced itself out of the market, but most of the panel fences will give you a good job and are much easier to erect.

I'm afraid that the trouble Michael experienced with his existing fence is simply a case of getting what he paid for. Interwoven panels are the cheapest available and are made by weaving thin timber laths on to a frame — in his case, obviously too thin. If you are buying interwoven fencing it is an economy in the long run to go for a really good quality panel with laths at least ⅜ inch thick.

There are many other types of panel on the market now, and unless you can afford feather-edge – and most folk can't – I would choose one with horizontal struts. Don't

necessarily go for the cheapest, either. It will pay you hands down to erect a fence that will last.

When pricing your fence don't forget to allow for the cost of the posts. You will need 3 inch by 3 inch timber, and they should be 2 feet longer than the height of the panel. You will generally need one more post than the number of panels.

Erection is a piece of cake. Start by marking the fence line with a string stretched tight from end to end. Make sure you get this absolutely right, bearing in mind that feuds between neighbours over even an inch or two of boundary are by no means uncommon. Now set the first post. This will need to be sunk 20 inches in the ground, leaving enough post out of the ground to allow the panel to be raised 2 inches above soil level, with a further 2 inches above the panel.

Set the post in a 6:1 mix of ballast and cement, well tamped down around it. Make quite sure that it is straight both ways by checking with a spirit level, and ensure that the inside edge just touches your marker line.

Now measure for the next hole, using either the panel itself or the panel capping. When the second hole has been dug to the correct depth, fix the panel to the first post. Use 3-inch nails, preferably galvanised, nailing both sides of the panel. The second post can now be set in the hole and nailed to the panel, then filled round with concrete. Check again with the spirit level for straightness both ways.

It is important that the panel should be strutted either side to support it while the concrete sets. Temporarily nail a piece of old timber to the top of the panel and wedge it firmly in the ground, without disturbing the alignment. Do not remove the struts until the concrete is quite hard. The remainder of the panels can now be erected in the same way.

As you proceed, it's not a bad idea just to cast your eye along the tops of the panels to make sure they are all still in line.

Unless you are lucky, when you get to the end of the run you will need a special panel. Put the final post in and measure accurately the size of panel required. Either get the manufacturer to make you a special size or, if you're handy with a saw and hammer, cut down a full-size panel. When all the panels are up and the concrete has set, finish off by nailing on the post and panel caps.

Since fencing panels are made in a rigid square, it is not possible to slope them. So if you have sloping ground you will need to 'step' the fencing. First work out how much of

Even if your garden is small and hemmed in you can increase the attraction by the addition of a patio and plants in containers.

a fall you have from end to end, which is easily done with a spirit level and straight edge. Divide the amount of fall by the number of panels to find the required drop at each post and don't forget that when you buy the posts they will need to be that much longer. For example, if on a 36-foot run the drop is 2 feet, each of the six panels will need to be dropped 4 inches.

Erect the first panel normally: it will then be 2 inches off the ground at one post, and 6 inches at the next. The second panel is then dropped 4 inches below the first, and so on. If the space at the bottom is too great it can be filled in with a gravel board (a piece of treated timber, 1 inch thick, nailed between the posts under the panel). This will have to be covered with soil at least at one end. Even if it does rot after a while, it is still much cheaper to replace than a panel.

Just one general word of warning when erecting a panel fence. Never, never put the posts in first and hope to fit the panels to them. You need only be half-an-inch out and, whether the gap is too wide or too narrow, you're in trouble, especially in these days of metrication. All too often panels that are referred to as '6 feet long' turn out to be what is known as a 'metric 6 feet'. That's about an eighth of an inch shorter. No wonder the Europeans think we're odd!

While I'm dispensing words of warning, I feel I should chastise Michael for his enthusiasm with the creosote brush. What he is doing is treating his fence with one of the most effective weedkillers known to man. Unfortunately its effect is total, so it will kill his dahlias as well as his docks. There are several other types of timber treatment that are not toxic to plant life.

That old ivy can be a problem, can't it? I think it looks marvellous on a wall, but there's little doubt that it does cause disintegration of the mortar. Other self-clinging climbers, such as Virginia creeper and the very attractive, white-flowered Hydrangea petiolaris, don't seem to cause so much damage. If you're worried about it, then why not stick to one of the other climbers that don't cling? Perhaps the most popular of these are the numerous varieties of clematis, roses, summer and winter jasmine, and the non-clinging variegated ivies. These will need some form of support and the simplest way is to nail and wire the wall. Alternatively there are plenty of plastic supports that will do the job very well.